THE CHRONICLES OF

CONAN

VOLUME 12

THE BEAST KING OF ABOMBI

AND OTHER STORIES

THE CHRONICLES OF
CONAN®

VOLUME 12

THE BEAST KING OF ABOMBI
AND OTHER STORIES

Based on the classic pulp
character Conan the Barbarian,
created by

ROBERT E. HOWARD

Written by

ROY THOMAS

Illustrated by

JOHN BUSCEMA
and others

Coloring by

PETER DAWES, DONOVAN YACIUK,
and **WIL GLASS** with **ALL THUMBS CREATIVE**

DARK HORSE BOOKS®

Publisher
MIKE RICHARDSON

Collection Designer
DARIN FABRICK

Art Director
LIA RIBACCHI

Collection Editors
JEREMY BARLOW,
MATT DRYER and **DAVE MARSHALL**

Special thanks to Fredrik Malmberg, Thommy Wojciechowski, and Leigh
Stone at Conan Properties; Arthur Lieberman at Lieberman & Norwalk,
LLP; Marco Lupoi at Panini; Scott Allie, Kurt Busiek, Lance Kreiter
and Roy Thomas.

This volume collects issues ninety-one and ninety-three through one hundred of the
Marvel comic-book series **Conan the Barbarian.**

Published by Dark Horse Books
A division of Dark Horse Comics, Inc.
10956 SE Main Street
Milwaukie, OR 97222

www.darkhorse.com
www.conan.com

To find a comics shop in your area, call the Comic Shop Locator Service
toll-free at 1-888-266-4226

First edition: July 2007
ISBN-10: 1-59307-778-5
ISBN-13: 978-1-59307-778-5

1 3 5 7 9 10 8 6 4 2

Printed in China

TABLE OF CONTENTS

ALL STORIES WRITTEN BY ROY THOMAS

"Know, O prince, that between the years when the oceans drank Atlantis and the gleaming cities, and the rise of the sons of Aryas, there was an Age undreamed of, when shining kingdoms lay spread across the world like blue mantles beneath the stars.

"Hither came Conan, the Cimmerian, black-haired, sullen-eyed, sword in hand, a thief, a reaver, a slayer, with gigantic melancholies and gigantic mirth, to tread the jeweled thrones of the Earth under his sandaled feet."

—*The Nemedian Chronicles.*

STan Lee PRESENTS: **CONAN THE BARBARIAN**™

SAVAGE DOINGS IN SHEM!

SOMEWHERE ON THE COAST OF STYGIA, SOUTH OF KHEMI--

A THIN, SHIMMERING SHORE-LINE IS ALL THAT HOLDS THE WEST-ERN OCEAN FROM THE SWAMPY, VERMIN-INFESTED STYGIAN MARSHES.

AND, ON THAT SHORE, A TRIO OF HEROIC BUT WEARY FIGURES WAIT WITH VARYING DEGREES OF PATIENCE, AS A LONGBOAT IS LOWERED FROM A SHIP ANCHORED NOT FAR DISTANT...

HAIL, BÊLIT! HAIL AMRA!

HAIL YOURSELF, MY CORSAIRS-- AND KEEP THOSE OARS MOVING!

ISHTAR-- BUT AFTER ALL THESE WEEKS ON LAND, IT WILL FEEL GOOD TO HAVE THE DECKS OF THE TIGRESS BENEATH MY FEET AGAIN!

I ONLY HOPE THAT I, IN TURN, DON'T TURN OUT TO HAVE A TEN-DENCY TOWARD SEASICKNESS.

AS THE FLYING HAWKS OF HARAKHT MADE YOU AIR-SICK, AS YOU CALLED IT?

DON'T WORRY, ZULA. AFTER ALL...

WE CAN ALWAYS TOSS YOU OFF THE SHIP, eh?

ROY THOMAS
WRITER/EDITOR

JOHN BUSCEMA & ERNIE CHAN
ILLUSTRATORS

TOM ORZECHOWSKI
letterer

JIM SHOOTER
CONSULTING EDITOR

FEATURING CHARACTERS CREATED BY ROBERT E. HOWARD

SOON... **N'YAGA! I THANK THE GODS YOU ARE WELL AGAIN, MY MENTOR!**

I WIN EVERY BATTLE BUT THE ONE WITH AGE, GODDESS. *

*UNDER N'YAGA'S TUTELAGE, THE BLACK CORSAIRS REVERE BÊLIT AS THE DAUGHTER OF THEIR DEATH-GODDESS DERKETA. --Roy.

BUT, I DON'T SEE ONE FACE I'VE MISSED, OF LATE.

WHERE IS M'GORA, MY SUB-CHIEF?

OH, YOU KNOW HOW YOUNG MEN ARE, GODDESS... EVER RESTLESS.

HE'LL BE ALONG PRESENTLY.

AH, AMRA-- I TRUST THERE ARE MANY STYGIAN WOMEN WAILING, MATE-LESS, BECAUSE OF YOUR BLADE.

ONE OR TWO, LARANGA.

BUT NOW, I'VE SOMEONE I WANT YOU CORSAIRS TO MEET...

THIS IS ZULA, A MAN OF THE ZAMBALLAHS WHO'LL BE JOINING US FOR A TIME.

HE IS WELCOME. BUT-- I KNOW THE NAME ZAMBALLAH.

WAS THAT TRIBE NOT SLAIN, TO A MAN, SOME YEARS AGO?

TO A MAN, YES-- BUT A BOY NAMED ZULA WAS SOLD INTO STYGIAN SLAVERY.

NOW, THAT BOY IS GROWN TO MANHOOD-- AND WANTS NOTHING SO MUCH AS REVENGE UPON CERTAIN STYGIANS.

WHEN SWORDS ARE DRAWN ABOARD THE TIGRESS, I TRUST YOU'LL FIND MINE AS SHARP AS ANY.

ZULA DOES NOT MENTION... HIS OTHER RESOURCES.

ERE LONG, BENEATH NO LIGHT SAVE A *FULL*, WIDE-STARING MOON, AN *EERIE SOUND* IS HEARD.

IT'S THE *SOUND OF DRUMS*, THRUM-THRUMMING...

AND THE SOUND IS STRANGE AND *EERIE*, COMING AS IT DOES *NOT* FROM THE GREEN FASTNESS OF THE SAVAGE *JUNGLE* SO NEAR AT HAND...

...BUT FROM THE *DECKS OF THE TIGRESS!*

THE *BLACK CORSAIRS* ARE CELEBRATING THE RETURN OF THEIR *GODDESS*...

...WHO JUST HAPPENS TO BE LIKEWISE THE *CAPTAIN* OF THEIR MUCH-FEARED PIRATE SHIP.

WITH *WILD ABANDON* THE EBON BODIES SWAY MADLY...

...AS *SONGS* ARE CHANTED WHICH SEEM AS OLD AS THE *AGELESS FOREST* ITSELF.

FOR AN HOUR OR MORE, THE REVELRY *CONTINUES*...

THEN, *ZULA* DECIDES, AT CONAN'S URGING, TO SHOW *HIS* WARES--

LOOK CLOSELY, *DEEPLY* INTO MY EYES, BASARA! YOU ARE GROWING *SLEEPY*... YOUR EYELIDS *HEAVY*...

YES... SLEEPY...

GOOD. NOW, YOU THINK YOU HAVE ALWAYS BEEN A *MAN*, BASARA...

...BUT YOU ARE *WRONG*.

YOU ARE *NOT* A MAN AT ALL, BUT... A *BIRD*.

A *SEAGULL*, FIT TO SOAR ACROSS THE *OCEAN*, TO LANDS *UNSEEN* BY MORTAL EYE!

DO YOU *HEAR* ME, BASARA?

AWWKK

HE *HEARS* YOU, ZAMBALLAH!

AYE-- AND TRIES TO FLY LIKE A SQUAWKING *GULL!*

AWK AWK

BASARA-- *DON'T*--!

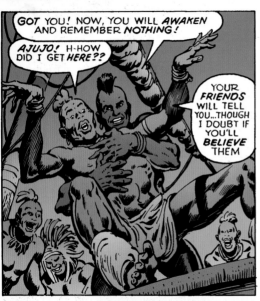

GOT YOU! NOW, YOU WILL *AWAKEN* AND REMEMBER *NOTHING!*

AJUJO! H-HOW DID I GET *HERE??*

YOUR *FRIENDS* WILL TELL YOU...THOUGH I DOUBT IF YOU'LL *BELIEVE* THEM

IT'S *GOOD* TO REVEL THUS A WHILE, eh. BÊLIT? THE *LAST* TIME WE DID SO, IT WAS SPOILED BY THE *RIVER-DRAGONS.**

IT WAS THE *WENCH* YOU DANCED WITH THAT SPOILED IT FOR *ME!*

THUS, TO REMIND YOU WHAT *REAL* DANCING IS--

*ISSUE #60. --Roy.

--LOOK TO *BÊLIT,* QUEEN OF THE *BLACK COAST!*

INSTANTLY, HER GRINNING CORSAIRS *FALL* IN WITH THE SHEMITE'S SINUOUS, SENSUOUS DANCE...

...AND CONAN IS REMINDED OF THE *LOVE-DANCE* SHE DID FOR HIM, ON THE DAY THREE YEARS GONE WHEN THEY FIRST *MET...*

...A DAY HE HAD EXPECTED TO *TASTE* STEEL INSTEAD!

SHE DANCES **AGAIN** AS SHE DANCED **THAT DAY**--

--A DANCE OF PRIMITIVE **PASSION** AND MAD **ABANDON**--

-- LIKE THE URGE OF **CREATION**, AND THE URGE OF **DEATH**.

NO LONGER IS SHE THE **BLOOD-MAD SHE-PIRATE**, WILD FOR **REVENGE** ON THE USURPERS OF HER RIGHTFUL **THRONE**...

...OR EVEN FOR THE **BETRAYAL** OF HER KINGLY **FATHER**...

...BUT MERELY A **WOMAN**...

...AN **ELEMENTAL**, **PRIMEVAL WOMAN**...

...A **WOMAN** IN **LOVE!**

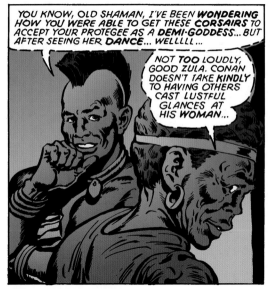

YOU KNOW, OLD SHAMAN, I'VE BEEN **WONDERING** HOW YOU WERE ABLE TO GET THESE **CORSAIRS** TO ACCEPT YOUR PROTEGEE AS A **DEMI-GODDESS**... BUT AFTER SEEING HER **DANCE**... WELLLLL...

NOT **TOO** LOUDLY, GOOD ZULA. CONAN DOESN'T TAKE **KINDLY** TO HAVING OTHERS CAST LUSTFUL GLANCES AT HIS **WOMAN**...

STRANGE! I, HAVING BEEN HER TUTOR WHEN SHE WAS KNEE-HIGH TO A BAT-SQUIRREL...

...STILL THINK OF HER AS THE **ROYAL CHILD** SHE WAS BACK IN **ASGALUN.**

...WHILE CONAN, OBVIOUSLY...

...SEES HER...

...QUITE DIFFERENTLY...!

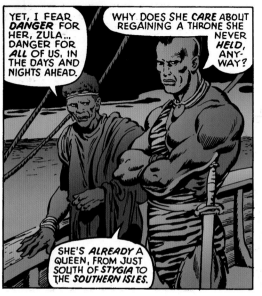

YET, I FEAR **DANGER** FOR HER, ZULA... DANGER FOR **ALL** OF US, IN THE DAYS AND NIGHTS AHEAD.

WHY DOES SHE **CARE** ABOUT REGAINING A THRONE SHE NEVER **HELD,** ANY-WAY?

SHE'S **ALREADY** A QUEEN, FROM JUST SOUTH OF **STYGIA** TO THE **SOUTHERN ISLES.**

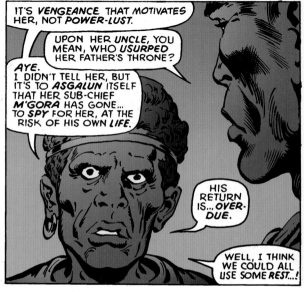

IT'S **VENGEANCE** THAT MOTIVATES HER, NOT **POWER-LUST.**

UPON HER **UNCLE,** YOU MEAN, WHO **USURPED** HER FATHER'S THRONE?

AYE. I DIDN'T TELL HER, BUT IT'S TO **ASGALUN** ITSELF THAT HER SUB-CHIEF **M'GORA** HAS GONE... TO **SPY** FOR HER, AT THE RISK OF HIS OWN **LIFE.**

HIS RETURN IS... **OVER-DUE.**

WELL, I THINK WE COULD ALL USE SOME REST...!

12

MORNING-- SOMBRE GRAY SHADOWS GIVE WAY SLOWLY TO A GROWING, VERDANT RADIANCE...

...THOUGH THERE'S ONLY **ONE** AWAKE TO SEE IT, AT FIRST.

THEN, A **SECOND** FIGURE STEPS ONTO THE TIGRESS' DECKS...

...TO STRETCH AND YAWN LIKE SOME **BRONZE PANTHER** IN THE RISING BLACK-COAST SUN.

YET, ALREADY, THERE IS A **CLEARNESS** AND A **VIBRANCY** IN SMOLDERING BLUE EYES WHICH FEW **CIVILIZED** MEN, JUST RISEN FROM THEIR BEDS, COULD MATCH.

A FEW SECONDS MORE, AND HE IS **NOT ALONE**... THOUGH SHE WHO JOINS HIM IS AS UNSPEAKING AS HE...

...NOR CAN **WORDS** DO ANYTHING BUT **SPOIL** CERTAIN MOMENTS... CERTAIN MOODS--

AS WITNESS--

GODDESS! AMRA!

M'GORA COMES!!

M'GORA!? NOW WHERE THE DEVIL WAS HE--?

CONAN-- LOOK!

13

IT'S M'GORA, ALL RIGHT--BUT HE'LL NEVER MAKE IT TO THE *SHIP!*

SWAMP RATS!!

SHREEEEEE

HO, *CORSAIRS!* RISE AND *EARN YOUR KEEP!*

M'GORA'S BACK--AND HE'S GOT *COMPANY!*

THROW ME A *SWORD, DOGS--* AND *HURRY!*

MEANWHILE, BÊLIT'S SUB-CHIEFTAIN PROVES THAT, THOUGH THE SPEAR IS HIS NATURAL WEAPON, HE IS NO SLOUCH WITH A SWORD...

BUT, IN THE ACT OF PIERCING ONE OF THE SABRE-FANGED RODENTS, THE BLADE CATCHES-- LEAVING HIM WEAPONLESS--

--THOUGH HARDLY FRIENDLESS.

GUARD YOUR *EYES,* M'GORA!

WE'LL BE THERE BEFORE THEY CAN *OVER-WHELM* YOU!

WHETHER IN HYBORIAN TIMES OR THE PRESENT, PERHAPS THE THING MOST FEARED ABOUT ANY KIND OF RAT--

REEE*K*

--IS THAT IT SEEMS TO KNOW NO KIND OF FEAR, ITSELF.

YET, THE *SAME* COULD BE SAID FOR THE *BLACK* CORSAIRS--

--AND FOR SHE WHOM THEY WOULD *FOLLOW* INTO THE *BRIGHTEST BURNING HELL.*

SHREEEE

AND, IF *ZULA* CANNOT EMPLOY HIS *VAUNTED HYPNOTISM* ON THESE *OVERSIZED VERMIN*--

--HE SHOWS THAT HE LEARNED *OTHER* THINGS WHILE A *SLAVE* IN MAGIC-RIDDEN *KHESHATTA.*

FINALLY, AS THE *SURVIVING* RATS RELUCTANTLY FLEE BLEEDING INTO THE *SWAMP,* WHERE THEY WILL SOON BE TEARING ONLY AT *EACH OTHER...*

CROM! LET'S GET OUT OF HERE, BEFORE THEIR MAD *COURAGE* RETURNS!

WE'LL TALK ON *BOARD.*

THUS, ERE LONG...

N'YAGA SHOULD HAVE *TOLD* ME WHERE YOU HAD GONE, M'GORA.

I ASKED HIM *NOT* TO, GODDESS.

I WISHED TO *LEARN* WHAT I COULD OF THE WAY THINGS ARE IN *ASGALUN...*

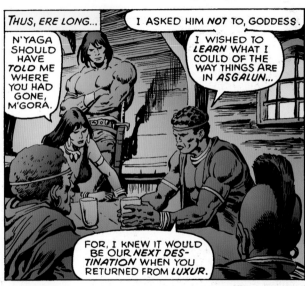

FOR, I KNEW IT WOULD BE OUR *NEXT DESTINATION* WHEN YOU RETURNED FROM *LUXUR.*

AND *DID* YOU?

AYE, GODDESS! AND SPIDERS WEAVE *SIMPLE WEBS,* COMPARED TO THOSE WAITING TO *SNARE* YOU IN THE CITY OF YOUR *FATHER,* WHO MATED WITH *DERKETA.*

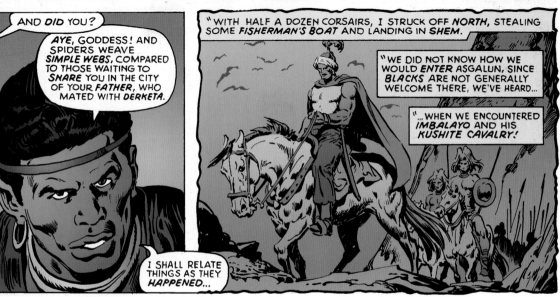

"WITH HALF A DOZEN CORSAIRS, I STRUCK OFF *NORTH,* STEALING SOME *FISHERMAN'S BOAT* AND LANDING IN *SHEM.*

"WE DID NOT KNOW HOW WE WOULD *ENTER* ASGALUN, SINCE *BLACKS* ARE NOT GENERALLY WELCOME THERE, WE'VE HEARD...

"...WHEN WE ENCOUNTERED *IMBALAYO* AND HIS *KUSHITE CAVALRY!*

I SHALL RELATE THINGS AS THEY *HAPPENED...*

"TELLING THEM WE WERE BUT *LOST WANDERERS* FROM AFAR SOUTH, WE LEARNED THEY WERE ON THEIR WAY TO *ASGALUN* ITSELF.

"THEY GAVE US A CHOICE: *JOIN* THEIR CAVALRY, OR THEY WOULD *SLAY* US THEN AND THERE FOR OUR *WEAPONS*.

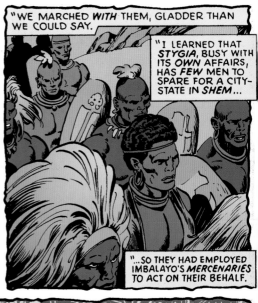

"WE MARCHED *WITH* THEM, GLADDER THAN WE COULD SAY.

"I LEARNED THAT *STYGIA*, BUSY WITH ITS *OWN* AFFAIRS, HAS *FEW* MEN TO SPARE FOR A CITY-STATE IN *SHEM*...

"...SO THEY HAD EMPLOYED *IMBALAYO'S MERCENARIES* TO ACT ON THEIR BEHALF.

"NOT MANY DAYS AFTERWARD, WE MARCHED INTO *ASGALUN*.

"IT WAS THE *FIRST* SHEMITISH CITY WE HAD EVER SEEN... FROM THE *INSIDE*.

"YET, IT WAS NOT THE GREAT SEVEN-TIERED *ZIGGURAT* WHICH TOWERS OVER THE CITY WHICH MOST CAUGHT MY EYE THAT DAY...

"... BUT THE SIGHT, IN A ROYAL PARADE, OF *KING NIM-KARRAK*, HE WHOM YOU *HATE* MORE THAN ANY OTHER.

"THOUGH HE'S A *SHEMITE*, HIS GUARDS WERE ALL *STYGIANS*..."

... AND HE SEEMED MORE A *PRISONER* THAN A *MONARCH*.

HE'LL SEEM A *CORPSE*, WHEN MY SWORD GETS WITHIN STRIKING-RANGE OF HIS *BELLY!* GO ON.

STYGIAN INFLUENCE IS *EVERY-WHERE* IN ASGALUN, GODDESS.

"A FEW DAYS LATER, A TROOP OF RIDERS-- *HYRKANIANS*, WE LEARNED--ARRIVED FROM THE *EAST*... CALLED, IT SEEMS, BY *NIM-KARRAK* IN SECRET.

"FROM THAT HOUR, *ONLY HYRKANIANS* APPEARED WITH THE KING OR GUARDED HIS PALACE... AND I WONDERED *WHY*.

"FROM A DRUNKEN *STYGIAN*, I LEARNED OF RUMORS THAT STYGIA MAY BE ABOUT TO *CLAIM* THE CITY OUTRIGHT... EVEN THOUGH THAT WOULD DOUBTLESS CAUSE *CIVIL WAR* AMONG THE SHEMITE POPULATION.

"THAT IS MOST LIKELY WHY *IMBALAYO* AND HIS MEN WERE ADDED TO THE STYGIAN GARRISON.

"MEANWHILE, THE ONLY MAN IN THE CITY BESIDES NIM-KARRAK WHO CLAIMS NOBLE BLOOD IS *URIAZ*... A FAT, BEARDED OAF WHO SEEMS CONTENT TO LOLL IN HIS *PLEASURE GARDEN*.

"BUT, PERHAPS HE MERELY *PRETENDS*... TO SAVE HIS *LIFE*.

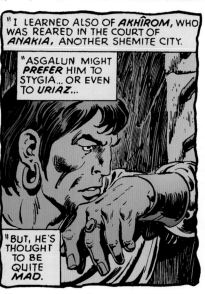

"I LEARNED ALSO OF *AKHIROM*, WHO WAS REARED IN THE COURT OF *ANAKIA*, ANOTHER SHEMITE CITY.

"ASGALUN MIGHT *PREFER* HIM TO STYGIA... OR EVEN TO *URIAZ*...

"BUT, HE'S THOUGHT TO BE QUITE *MAD*.

"STILL, IT'S SAID HE'S TAKEN LATELY AN INTEREST IN THE TROOPS OF *KING SUMUABI OF ANAKIA*, AND EVEN NOW LEADS AN ARMY *SOMEWHERE* IN SHEM...

"AND *WHO KNOWS?* IF THINGS GET *BAD* ENOUGH IN ASGALUN, IT MIGHT BE TO *HIS*-- AND *ANAKIA'S*-- BENEFIT...!"

I HOPE *YOU* CAN MAKE SENSE OF ALL I'VE TOLD YOU, GODDESS... AND AMRA... FOR I VOW, IT MAKES MY *HEAD* SPIN.

YOU'RE *NOT* AS SIMPLE AS YOU *PRETEND*, GOOD M'GORA.

BY THE WAY, I'M *ZULA*... LATE OF *KHESHATTA*.

WELL? WHAT *THINK* YOU, MY FRIENDS?

M'GORA HAS DONE *WELL*-- BUT *BY CROM!* CIVILIZED MEN DO MORE *PLOTTING* THAN *SLEEPING*, IT SEEMS!

AYE! ALL THE MONARCHS IN SHEM ARE *RELATED*, MORE OR LESS-- WHICH MAKES THEIR *WARS* ALL THE MORE *BITTER*.

NO MATTER-- ASGALUN'S THRONE IS *MINE ALONE*...

... AND *NIM-KARRAK*, DAMN HIM, MUST *DIE!*

AGREED--AND I TOO HAVE REVENGE WAITING FOR ME IN THAT CITY!

STILL, WE MUST ACT CAUTIOUSLY...

YOU HEARD WHAT M'GORA SAID-- THE STYGIANS PLAN TO ANNEX ASGALUN... PERHAPS ALL THE PROVINCE OF PELISHTIA!

THEN WHERE WILL BE THE GAIN FROM CAUTION?

YOUR NEW FRIEND ZULA SPEAKS WORDS OF WISDOM, BÊLIT

WE MUST ACT SLOWLY-- BUILD UP ALLIES IN THE CITIES AROUND ASGALUN, AND ONLY THEN--

NO! I'LL NOT TAKE THE CHANCE!

I MOVE OUT TOMORROW-- EVEN IF I MUST GO ALONE!

CONAN, CAN'T YOU REASON WITH HER? PERHAPS, IF YOU REFUSED TO ACCOMPANY HER...

I HAVE VOWED TO HELP HER GAIN VENGEANCE, ZULA.

WHERE SHE GOES, I GO.

AND, DESPITE GRAVE MISGIVINGS, THE SAME PROVES TRUE OF M'GORA AND ZULA AS WELL.

WHILE THE TIGRESS STAYS AT SEA, A PARTY OF FOUR SOON TREAD THE COASTS OF SHEM, IN THE PROVINCE CALLED PELISHTIA...

...TILL, NOT MANY DAYS AFTERWARD, THE GATES OF ASGALUN COMES INTO VIEW.

HALT AND IDENTIFY YOURSELVES, WAYFARERS!

I AM M'GORA... AND I RETURN FROM A MISSION ON WHICH I WAS SENT BY IMBALAYO, GENERAL OF THE KUSHITES!

YES, I REMEMBER SEEING YOU WITH THEM-- BUT WE RECEIVED NO WORD THAT--

BY AJUJO, MAN--MUST I CALL IMBALAYO AND HIS MEN, SIMPLY TO BRING THESE ADVISORS TO HIM?

HE'LL NOT LIKE THAT!

HOW DO WE KNOW HE SENT YOU FORTH? WHO VOUCHES FOR YOU FROM WITHIN THE GATE?

I DO! I, YASUNGA, AND THESE *WITH* ME!

MORE KUSHITES-- WEARING THE HEADDRESS OF IMBALAYO'S WARRIORS!

LET THEM *PASS*, IF IMBALAYO'S OWN SPEAK FOR THEM!

AYE-- BUT NEXT TIME, HE SHOULD *INFORM* THE GATE OF YOUR COMINGS AND GOINGS!

IMBALAYO IS AN *ALLY* OF YOU STYGIANS-- BUT HE, AND THUS WE, ANSWER TO *NO* STYGIAN BELOW THE RANK OF *COMMANDER!*

YOU DID *WELL,* YASUNGA.

WE BUT DID WHAT YOU *BADE* US, M'GORA.

WE MADE FAKE *HEADDRESSES,* TO LOOK LIKE TRUE KUSHITES...

...THEN WAITED IN SHADOWS NEAR THE GATE, EVERY THIRD *NOON,* FOR YOUR *RETURN.*

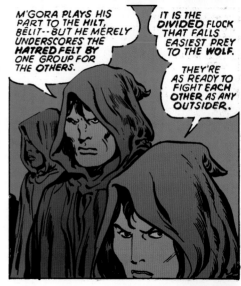

M'GORA PLAYS HIS PART TO THE *HILT,* BÉLIT-- BUT HE MERELY *UNDERSCORES* THE *HATRED* FELT BY ONE GROUP FOR THE OTHERS.

IT IS THE *DIVIDED* FLOCK THAT FALLS EASIEST PREY TO THE *WOLF.*

THEY'RE AS READY TO *FIGHT EACH OTHER* AS ANY *OUTSIDER.*

PARDON, *GODDESS...* AND *AMRA...* BUT WE MUST HIDE THESE *FALSE* HEADDRESSES, AND RETURN TO THE KUSHITE *BARRACKS,* BEFORE WE ARE MISSED.

THE PALACE, AS YOU KNOW, IS BEYOND THE *GREAT ZIGGURAT...* AND M'GORA CAN HELP KEEP YOU CLEAR OF THE *REAL* KUSHITES.

MY THANKS, YASANGA!

THEN, AS THE DIS-GUISED QUARTET CONTINUE THROUGH THE STREETS OF THIS CITY WHERE BÉLIT WAS *BORN...*

THEY SEE THE RECENTLY ARRIVED *HYRKANIANS*... HIRELINGS OF *NIM-KARRAK*, DISTRUSTED BY ONE AND ALL... UNDER A SELDOM-SEEN GENERAL NAMED *MAZDAK*...

...THE DUSKY *STYGIANS*, RESTIVE AFTER WHAT AMOUNTS TO A *DECADE'S OCCUPATION* OF THIS CITY WHICH LOVES THEM *NOT*...

...AND THE *KUSHITES*, NOMINALLY THE *ALLIES* OF THE STYGIANS, YET DISTRUSTED BY THEM AS MUCH AS BY THE HYRKANIANS... OR THE *POPULACE*.

THE *POPULACE!* THAT IS WHAT CONCERNS CONAN *MOST*.

WHAT DO THEY WANT-- AND WHOSE *SIDE* WILL THEIR VAST NUMBERS FAVOR, IF *CIVIL WAR* ERUPTS BETWEEN THE VARIOUS FOREIGN FACTIONS?

CERTAINLY THEY WOULD FAVOR ANOTHER SHEM-ITE RULER, IF *NIM-KARRAK FALLS*...

BUT, WOULD THEY RECOG-NIZE *BÉLIT* AS SUCH... ESPEC-IALLY IF SHE *ASSASSINATES* NIM-KARRAK, AS SHE PLANS?

ABRUPTLY, A SMALL *CONFRON-TATION* BETWEEN M'GORA AND A *REAL* KUSHITE WARRIOR INTERRUPTS THE CIMMERIAN'S THOUGHTS...

YOU! WHERE ARE YOU *TAKING* THESE THREE?

TO THE *GARDEN* WHERE IMBALAYO *AWAITS* THEM!

I TAKE THE RESPONSI-BILITY-- DO NOT *WORRY* YOURSELF ABOUT IT!

WHERE IN ISHTAR'S NAME *ARE* WE GOING, M'GORA?

ALMOST WHERE I *SAID*, GODDESS.

TO A *PLEASURE GARDEN* COMMAN-DEERED BY IMBALAYO, BUT SELDOM *USED* BY HIM.

IT WILL PROVE A GOOD *ENTRANCE* TO THE PALACE, TO TAKE NIM-KARRAK *UNAWARES.*

PLEASURE GARDEN? IT'S BEEN *YEARS* SINCE I WAS A CHILD IN ASGALUN, TRUE -- BUT I REMEMBER NO SUCH...

IT HAS BEEN *NEWLY ADDED,* GODDESS.

IT LIES IN THE VERY *SHADOW* OF THE *GREAT ZIGGURAT* --

-- *RIGHT* THROUGH *YONDER DOOR!*

GOOD! NO ONE IN *SIGHT!*

ENTER, BUT KEEP *NEAR* ME --

-- WHILE I *LOCK* THE THICK DOOR BEHIND US!

BREATHING! DO YOU *HEAR* IT, *BÊLIT* -- *ZULA?*

THAT I *DO!* BUT, YOUR MAN M'GORA WOULDN'T HAVE *BETRAYED* US, WOULD HE?

NEVER! HE IS AS *LOYAL* AS --

WAIT! LOOK!

STYGIANS!

THROW DOWN YOUR *WEAPONS,* INTRUDERS -- OR *DIE!*

BY ORDER OF *NIM-KARRAK,* KING OF *ASGALUN!*

I'LL PERISH WITH *STEEL* IN MY BELLY BEFORE I'LL SURRENDER TO *THAT SWINE!*

KEEP HARD AGAINST THE *WALL,* WOMAN!

WE'LL TAKE MANY OF THESE SNAKE-LOVERS *WITH US* ERE WE FALL!

SWORDS ALONE WON'T HELP! WE'RE HOPELESSLY *OUTNUMBERED!*

BUT, PERHAPS A FEW *MYSTIC GESTURES* LEARNED IN *KHESHATTA* WILL HELP --

PERHAPS THEY *WOULD,* ZAMBALLAH...

...BUT YOU'LL **NOT** USE THEM!

AARRH

M'GORA!? BUT-- IT ISN'T **POSSIBLE**!

DON'T WASTE YOUR **BREATH**, WOMAN!

KEEP FIGHTING! IT'S JUST THE **TWO** OF US NOW!

AYE, BUT THERE AREN'T **THAT MANY** OF THESE DOGS! MAYBE--

NEXT MOMENT, BÊLIT'S FLEETING VISIONS OF VICTORY OR ESCAPE ARE **SMOTHERED** BENEATH--

A NET!!

THEN THEY'VE BEEN **WAITING** FOR US-- **ALL ALONG!**

I **KNEW** THINGS HAD GONE TOO EASILY, DAMN ME FOR A FOOL!

HACK AWAY AT THE **STRANDS**, MY LOVER, AND WE CAN STILL --

NO. IT'S **NO USE**.

WE'LL LEARN MORE IF WE **SURRENDER**-- SINCE THEY SEEM **NOT** TO INTEND TO **SLAY** US AT THE MOMENT.

THAT'S **TRUE**, BARBARIAN...

...THOUGH ONLY AS LONG AS **I** FAIL TO **TELL** THEM TO DO SO!

PTOR-NUBIS!*

OF COURSE! **THOTH-AMON** WARNED ME OF YOUR **IMMINENT** COMING.

*STYGIAN COUNCILOR TO NIM-KARRAK, AS SEEN IN VARIOUS ISSUES. -- R.T.

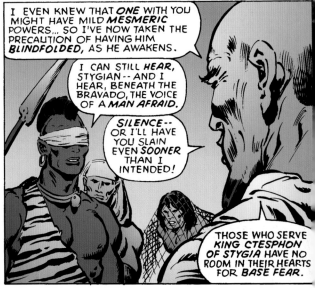

I EVEN KNEW THAT **ONE** WITH YOU MIGHT HAVE MILD **MESMERIC** POWERS... SO I'VE NOW TAKEN THE PRECAUTION OF HAVING HIM **BLINDFOLDED**, AS HE AWAKENS.

I CAN STILL **HEAR**, STYGIAN-- AND I HEAR, BENEATH THE BRAVADO, THE VOICE OF A **MAN AFRAID**.

SILENCE-- OR I'LL HAVE YOU SLAIN EVEN **SOONER** THAN I INTENDED!

THOSE WHO SERVE **KING CTESPHON OF STYGIA** HAVE NO ROOM IN THEIR HEARTS FOR **BASE FEAR**.

22

GODDESS! AMRA! FORGIVE ME, I PRAY YOU!

THOUGH I STRUCK THE ZAMBALLAH, I DO NOT KNOW WHAT MADE ME DO IT! I--

I KNOW, M'GORA... AND I HOLD YOU BLAMELESS!

PTOR-NUBIS, WEAK WIZARD THAT HE IS, POSSESSES ONLY ONE POWER--

TO TOUCH A MAN OR THING, AND BE OBEYED BY THAT WHICH HE HAS TOUCHED!

HE MADE YOU FORGET HIS ENCOUNTER WITH YOU...

...TILL YOU PICKED UP THE ROCK TO STRIKE ZULA.

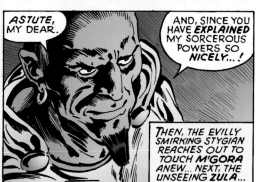

ASTUTE, MY DEAR.

AND, SINCE YOU HAVE EXPLAINED MY SORCEROUS POWERS SO NICELY...!

THEN, THE EVILLY SMIRKING STYGIAN REACHES OUT TO TOUCH M'GORA ANEW... NEXT, THE UNSEEING ZULA...

... AND, AT LAST, CONAN AND BÊLIT.

THERE! NOW YOU ARE ALL FOUR IN MY THRALL, THOUGH YOU DO NOT FEEL SO... FOR THE MOMENT.

PULL THE NET OFF THEM, DOGS--

--THAT THEY MAY FIGHT TO THE DEATH, AMONG THEMSELVES--

-- FOR THE GREATER GLORY OF KING CTESPHON III --AND FOR THOTH-AMON, MASTER MAGE OF THE BLACK RING!

NOR SHALL ANY OF YE PUT ASIDE YOUR SWORDS AGAIN--

--TILL THEY ARE SHEATHED IN THE FLESH OF YOUR COMPANIONS!

SLOWLY, CONAN AND BÊLIT--M'GORA AND ZULA--STALK TOWARD EACH OTHER AS IF SEEING, IN THOSE BEFORE THEM, THEIR WORST FOES, FIT ONLY FOR SLAYING.

AND SOMEWHERE, THOUSANDS OF LEAGUES AWAY, THE WIZARD THOTH-AMON LAUGHS GRIMLY TO HIMSELF...!

NEXT ISSUE: THE THING IN THE CRYPT!

THEN, AFTER THAT TALE OF CONAN'S NORTHERN YOUTH-- SHOWDOWN IN ASGALUN!

Stan Lee Presents: CONAN THE BARBARIAN™

OF RAGE AND REVENGE!

TWO ISSUES AGO, WE LEFT CONAN AND BÊLIT-- ZULA AND M'GORA-- ALL SQUARED OFF TO BATTLE ONE ANOTHER TO THE DEATH, UNDER THE MYSTIC SWAY OF THE STYGIAN WIZARD PTOR-NUBIS, IN A GARDEN SOMEWHERE IN THE HEART OF SHEMITISH ASGALUN.

AND THEY'RE STILL AT IT--!

FIGHT, FOOLS-- FIGHT TILL YE ALL BE DEAD!

HE WHOM PTOR-NUBIS TOUCHES MUST OBEY HIS COMMANDS--

--AND PTOR-NUBIS HAS LAID HIS HANDS ON YOU ALL!

ROY THOMAS ✱ JOHN BUSCEMA & ERNIE CHAN
WRITER/EDITOR ✱ ILLUSTRATORS

TOM ORZECHOWSKI letterer

JIM SHOOTER CONSULTING EDITOR

FEATURING CHARACTERS AND CONCEPTS CREATED BY ROBERT E. HOWARD

IN GRIM SILENCE THEY JOIN SWORDS, THE CIMMERIAN AND THE SHEMITE SHE-PIRATE--

AND WHO CAN SAY WHAT DEMI-THOUGHTS FLOW LIKE SLUGGISH RIVERS THROUGH THEIR ENSORCELLED BRAINS?

YET, IF THEIR MINDS ARE SLOW--

--THEIR REFLEXES ARE NOT--

--NEITHER CONAN'S BRAWNY SWORD-ARM, NOR BÊLIT'S LITHE FORM!

WHY NOT LET US GUT THEM, AND BE DONE WITH IT, PTOR-NUBIS?

BECAUSE I PREFER TO DO IT THIS WAY! I LOST FACE WHEN THE TWO WHITE PIRATES ESCAPED ASGALUN MONTHS AGO!

--AND VENGEANCE SEEMS EVER CLOSER TO MY GRASP, WITH EACH PASSING SECOND!

CONAN'S STEEL-BLUE EYES ARE GLAZED NOW AS HE FIGHTS THIS WOMAN WHO IS HIS MATE...

...AND M'GORA, THE CORSAIR SUB-CHIEF WHO UNWILLINGLY LED HIS COMRADES INTO THIS TRAP, LIKEWISE WIELDS A SWORD LIKE SOME INSPIRED PUPPET.

BUT, IF THE STYGIAN WOULD LOOK MORE CLOSELY AT THE TIGER-CLAD BLACK NAMED ZULA--

--HE MIGHT BEHOLD A FELINE INTELLIGENCE, WHICH BURNS THERE, UNDIMMED BY THE SORCERER'S EARLIER TOUCH.

FOR, ZULA, LAST OF THE ZAMBALLAHS, SPENT LONG, SECRET NIGHTS STUDYING ARCANE MAGIC WHEN HE WAS A SLAVE IN STYGIA'S CITY OF MAGICIANS...

...AND TO SUCH A ONE, THE TOUCH OF PTOR-NUBIS COULD BE SHAKEN OFF, AS A DUCK SHEDS WATER.

NOW, AS ZULA ALLOWS M'GORA, THOUGH A LESSER SWORDSMAN, TO "FORCE" HIM BACK TOWARD THE BAND OF GRINNING STYGIANS--

--HE RECALLS BEING SOLD INTO SLAVERY AS A CHILD, BY A YOUNG WIZARD--

...A WIZARD NAMED PTOR-NUBIS!

DIE, YOU STYGIAN JACKAL!

DIE, AT THE HAND OF ONE YOU WRONGED!

AND, AS THAT LETHAL BLADE SWINGS A FINAL TIME UPWARD--

--IS IT THE SUDDEN SHOCK OF RECOGNITION WHICH SHINES LIKE A FLARING BEACON IN PTOR-NUBIS'S WIDE-STARING EYES?

WE SHALL NEVER KNOW.

AAARRRGH

PTOR-NUBIS IS DEAD!

THEN, LET US SLAY THE FOUR OUTLANDERS!

AYE! THEY'RE TOO DANGEROUS TO LIVE!

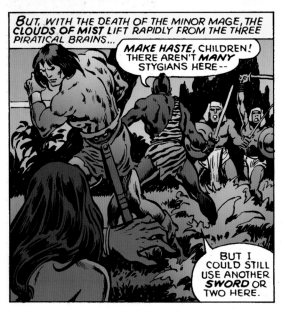

BUT, WITH THE DEATH OF THE MINOR MAGE, THE CLOUDS OF MIST LIFT RAPIDLY FROM THE THREE PIRATICAL BRAINS...

MAKE HASTE, CHILDREN! THERE AREN'T MANY STYGIANS HERE--

BUT I COULD STILL USE ANOTHER SWORD OR TWO HERE.

THEN YOU'LL HAVE THEM, ZULA!

YOU'VE WREAKED YOUR VENGEANCE, THEN, ON PTOR-NUBIS?

AYE-- THOUGH IT'S LEFT ME CURIOUSLY UNSATISFIED.

I BEGIN TO FEAR REVENGE IS NOT ALL IT'S CRACKED UP TO BE.

YOU'LL NOT HEAR *ME* SAY THAT, ZULA, WHEN I'VE SHEATHED MY SWORD IN *KING NIM-KARRAK'S BELLY!*

I'VE WAITED A *DECADE* AND MORE FOR MY REVENGE--AND THIS DAY, OR SOON, I SHALL *HAVE* IT!

WE *BELIEVE* YOU, WOMAN-- WE *BELIEVE* YOU!

BUT FIRST, LET'S KILL A FEW MORE *STYGIANS* BEFORE WE START IN ON *SHEMITE USURPERS,* eh?

NO *NEED,* CONAN.

WE'VE *WON!*

SO IT *SEEMS.*

WE'VE *NOT* WON-- NOT WHILE MY *TRAITOROUS UNCLE* STILL SITS THE THRONE!

OR *WORSE*--LET THE *STYGIANS* TAKE OVER THE CITY AND ANNEX IT AS PART OF THEIR *OWN* KINGDOM, AS WE'VE HEARD THEY MEAN TO DO!*

THEN YOU'D BEST ACT *QUICKLY,* WHILE THERE'S A SHEMITE CROWN TO *REGAIN.*

THAT I *SHALL*-- AND I KNOW THE *WAY.*

M'GORA-- I NEED *YOUR HELP* ON THIS....!

I AM YOURS TO *COMMAND,* GODDESS--IF YOU CAN FORGIVE ME FOR *BETRAYING* YOU.

YOU DID *NOT* BETRAY ME--YOU WERE MERELY *HYPNOTIZED.*

YOU ARE *KNOWN* HERE--AS A *KUSHITE MERCENARY.* SPREAD THE WORD THAT *ATRAHASIS'* DAUGHTERS HAS RETURNED TO CLAIM HER *THRONE!*

AYE!

I'LL GO *WITH* YOU, M'GORA... TO HELP YOU *FAN* THE RUMORS.

BUT, YOU LOOK EVEN *LESS* LIKE A TRUE KUSHITE THAN *I* DO...

YOU DO *NOT KNOW* WHITE MEN, MY FRIEND.

TO THEM, EVERY MAN SOUTH OF AQUILONIA LOOKS LIKE *EVERY OTHER.*

AND, ZULA PROVES IN THIS INSTANCE TO BE AS MUCH A **PROPHET** AS A **WARRIOR** OR A FLEDGLING **HYPNOTIST**-- AS HE AND M'GORA SPREAD THE WORD TO **SHEMITES**-- **KUSHITES**-- **HYRKANIANS**--

"THE **DAUGHTER OF ATRAHASIS** HAS RETURNED FROM EXILE-- AND WILL SOON **RECLAIM** HER RIGHTFUL THRONE FROM THE USURPER **NIM-KARRAK!**"

AND SPREAD IT **DOES**-- LIKE RIPPLES IN A SMALL POND.

EVEN THE SEVERAL BLACK **CORSAIRS** WHO HAVE ENLISTED IN THE ARMY OF THE KUSHITE MERCENARY **IMBALAYO** SPREAD THE WORD, TO ALL WHO WILL LISTEN.

WHILE, HIDING IN ONE OF THE CITY'S SEVERAL **PLEASURE GARDENS**...

TELL ME, **BÊLIT**-- DO YOU REALLY THINK THE **ASGALUNIM***★** CARE IF THEY ARE RULED BY **YOU**, OR **NIM-KARRAK**... OR THE **DEVIL**, FOR THAT MATTER?

NOT A **WHIT**-- SO LONG AS THE DEVIL'S A **SHEMITE!**

BUT, THERE'LL BE **HELL** TO PAY, IF THE **STYGIANS** FORMALLY ANNEX THE CITY.

★**PLURAL** FOR DWELLERS IN **ASGALUN**--Roy.

STILL, THEY'LL **ACCEPT** ME WHEN MY UNCLE'S DEAD-- BECAUSE, EXCEPT FOR FAT **URIAZ** OR THE MAD, WANDERING **AKHÎROM**, I'M THE ONLY PRETENDER WITH ROYAL **BLOOD** IN MY VEINS.

PERHAPS I SHOULD HAVE **CONTACTED** AKHÎROM, WHEREVER HE'S ROAMING WITH HIS ARMY-- MADE A **PACT** WITH HIM.

BUT, IT'S **TOO LATE** NOW! THE **DIE** IS **CAST!**

AND, IN THE EMERALD ROOM OF THE ROYAL PALACE, **KING NIM-KARRAK** HAS SUDDENLY MADE THE **SELFSAME** OBSERVATION...

PTOR-NUBIS IS DEAD-- HE **MUST** BE!

ELSE, HE WOULD HAVE **RETURNED** BY NOW, WITH **BÊLIT** AND HER LACKEYS IN TOW!

AND, IF THE **RUMORS** THAT THE STYGIANS INTEND TO **DETHRONE** ME TURN OUT TO BE **TRUE**--

THEY **ARE** TRUE, MAJESTY! ACCEPT THE WORD OF **SHYLA**! HE WHO IS YOUR **EARS!**

THEN-- I'VE **NO CHOICE** BUT TO ACT **QUICKLY**-- BEFORE **THEY** KNOW THAT **I** KNOW...!

COME, SHYLA! AT THIS JUNCTURE, I DARE NOT TRUST EVEN MY HIRED HYRKANIAN GUARDS.

THIS TUNNEL WILL LEAD US FROM THE THRONE ROOM-- TO A SAFE HAVEN--

--TILL WE CAN PLAN OUR NEXT MOVE!

AS IT TURNS OUT, NIM-KARRAK HAS A FAULTLESS SENSE OF TIMING...

THE SHEMITE KING IS GONE-- FLED!

HE MUST HAVE LEARNED WE MEANT TO IMPRISON HIM!

PRINCE KHAMUN! WE HAVE SCOURED THE WHOLE PALACE-- BUT NIM-KARRAK IS NOT TO BE FOUND!

SO! I AM IN ASGALUN ONLY A FEW HOURS-- AND ALREADY THINGS GO AWRY IN THIS SHEMITE FLESHPOT!

KING CTESPHON, WHO SENT ME HERE TO BE ITS MONARCH ON STYGIA'S BEHALF, WILL BE MOST DISPLEASED.

STILL, PERHAPS THERE'LL BE NO HARM DONE-- IF THE ANNOUNCEMENT OF MY KINGSHIP AND STYGIA'S ANNEXATION OF WHOLE PROVINCE COMES OFF AS SCHEDULED.

IT SHALL, O KHAMUN!

STILL, THERE IS ONE SMALL BLUE-BLOODED DETAIL TO TAKE CARE OF--

--THE MATTER OF... URIAZ...!

"URIAZ, NOBLEMAN OF ASGALUN -- FOR ALL OF NIM-KARRAK'S RULE, HE HAS BEEN CONTENT TO DALLY WITH HIS WINE AND HIS WOMEN IN HIS OWN PERSONAL PLEASURE GARDEN IN THE HEART OF THE CITY.

"NO LONGER, HOWEVER, CAN WE AFFORD TO HAVE HIM AT LARGE...

"... OR EVEN, PERHAPS, ALIVE!"

29

URIAZ IS **IN CUSTODY,** THEN, O PRINCE?

AYE-- FOR THE BRIEF TIME HE SHALL **EXIST** ON THIS EARTH, AT LEAST.

AND, WITH HIS **DEATH,** THERE'LL BE **NO MALE CLAIMANTS** TO THE THRONE LEFT IN **ALL PELISHTIA!**

SOME HOURS LATER, IN THE GREAT SQUARE, THE FATEFUL PROCLAMATION IS READ...

... AND, FROM THIS DAY FORWARD, **ASGALAN** SHALL EVER BE A CLIENT STATE OF **STYGIA...**

... UNDER **PRINCE KHAMUN,** ROYAL EMISSARY OF KING **CTESPHON III !**

A FEW OF THE **NATIVE SHEMITES** TAKE THE DREADED NEWS IN A WAY **NOT UNEXPECTED...**

NO! THERE'LL BE **NO FOREIGN YOKE** FOR **ASGALUN!**

DEATH TO THE STYGIANS!

... WHILE THE STYGIANS, IN TURN, REACT AS **THEY** MIGHT BE EXPECTED TO--

..., AND RUMORS OF A **FEMALE HEIR** WITHIN THE GATES ARE A BASE FALSEHOOD!

WE HAVE HERE, HOWEVER, **ONE** WHO IS AN **ENEMY OF PEACE** IN ASGALUN--

--THE NOBLEMAN **URIAZ,** COUSIN TO **NIM-KARRAK!**

HIS **EXECUTION** SHALL SIGNAL THE BEGINNING OF STYGIAN RULE IN PELISHTIA!

THEN, AT LAST, **PRINCE KHAMUN** HIMSELF STEPS FORWARD, HIS SEPULCHRAL TONES FILLING THE ACOUSTICALLY DESIGNED SQUARE...

MEN OF **ASGALUN!** I KNOW MANY OF YOU RESENT THE IMPOSITION OF STYGIAN RULE UPON THIS, YOUR CITY-- AND WE, IN TURN, RESENT ITS **NECESSITY!**

YET, YOU WILL DO YOURSELVES AND YOUR LOVED ONES A KINDNESS BY ACCEPTING OUR RULE-- SO THAT A TIME OF PEACE CAN SETTLE UPON THIS TROUBLED PROVINCE OF **PELISHTIA!**

THOSE WHO **OBEY** US WILL BE SUITABLY **REWARDED**--WHILE THOSE WHO **OPPOSE** US WILL NECESSARILY BE **PUNISHED!**

THE FORMER KING **NIM-KARRAK** HAS FLED, IN COWARDLY FASHION...

THOSE ASGALUNIM WHO HAVE **HEARD** OF URIAZ CARE **LITTLE** ABOUT HIM-- BUT WHO LIKES TO SEE HIS **COUNTRYMAN** PUT TO DEATH BY **FOREIGNERS**?

STILL, THEIR MURMURS OF PROTEST REMAIN JUST THAT-- **MURMURS**-- WHEN FACED WITH **STYGIAN SPEARS**...

... WHILE THE **HYRKANIANS**, PERSONALLY RECRUITED BY NIM-KARRAK, WATCH THE PROCEEDINGS **UNEASILY**.

AS THE FORMER SHEMITE KING'S PROTECTORS, WHAT WILL BE **THEIR** FATE--

--AT THE HANDS OF THE **STYGIANS** AND THEIR **KUSHITE MERCENARIES**?

THE **LATTER**, IN TURN, OBSERVE THE CEREMONY STOICALLY, SAYING **NOTHING**.

THEY ARE PAID IN **STYGIAN GOLD**... AND ARE **CONTENT**...

...THOUGH **MISTRUSTFUL**, IN THEIR WAY, OF **ALL** THE OTHER FACTIONS.

NOW, **BAL-YAMM**,... AS HIGH PRIEST OF ISHTAR IN ASGALUN, YOU WILL GIVE YOUR **BLESSINGS** TO THE TRANSFER OF AUTONOMY--

--ASSUMING, OF COURSE, YOU WISH TO LIVE TO **WITNESS** IT.

I... SHALL BRING THE **CROWN** OF PELISHTIA, O PRINCE.

BUT **REMEMBER**-- I HAVE BEEN PROMISED THAT **TEMPLES OF ISHTAR** SHALL STAND ALONGSIDE THOSE OF THE STYGIAN GOD **SET**.

IF IT **PLEASE** ME! NOW, THE **CROWN**, IF YOU WILL...

I HAVE IT **HERE**, O PRINCE.

GOOD! I WILL PLACE IT UPON **MY OWN HEAD**, WHILE THE GATHERING MOB STILL **GASPS** AT THE SIGHT OF **URIAZ'S** BEHEADING.

EXECUTIONER! PLACE THE **FAT ONE** ON THE **BLOCK**!

WORDLESSLY, THE HOODED, GREAT-MUSCLED EXECUTIONER DOES AS HE IS **BID**...

N-NO-- PLEASE! I DON'T **WANT** THE CROWN-- I SWEAR IT--!

IN ISHTAR'S NAME-- **LEAVE ME MY HEAD**, I BEG YOU!

SILENCE, PIG!

31

OFF WITH HIS HEAD, HOODSMAN-- NOW!

LET *ALL* ASGALUN KNOW WHAT IT MEANS TO DEFY HER *NEW PRINCE!*

I D-DEFIED *NO ONE!* P-PLEASE--!

Oh, YE GODS-- *PLEASE*--!

BELOW THE GREAT STEPS, TENSION RUNS LIKE A GROUNDED THUNDER-BOLT THROUGH THE SHEMITE CROWD...

NO! SPARE HIM!

LET *NO* SHEMITE BLOOD BE SHED BY *STYGIANS!*

I'LL DEAL WITH THAT RABBLE *LATER!*

HOODSMAN! DIDN'T YOU *HEAR* ME?

OFF WITH *HIS* HEAD-- OR I'LL HAVE YOUR *OWN!*

THE MASKED EXECUTIONER'S ONLY *ANSWER*--

--CRUSHES *BONES* AND ORGANS IN THE PRINCE'S SHATTERED RIB-CAGE, WHILE THE STYGIAN IS STILL LOOKING ON IN *STUNNED DISBELIEF*--

--TOO STARTLED EVEN TO *SCREAM* BEFORE HE DIES!

NOR SHALL HE EVER KNOW THAT HIS SLAYER IS THE ONE CALLED *CONAN*--

--OR *AMRA*, SINKER OF MANY A STYGIAN SHIP!

IT IS TIME WE *ENDED* THIS FARCE!

BÊLIT! SHOW YOUR-SELF!

MEN OF ASGALUN! BEHOLD BÊLIT-- TRUE DAUGHTER OF SLAUGHTERED KING ATRAHASIS--

--AND RIGHTFUL HEIR TO THE THRONE OF PELISHTIA!

THE GARMENTS OF A FEW *SLAIN* STYGIANS HAVE INDEED SERVED THE CORSAIRS *WELL*

DO YOU HEAR, SHEM-ITES?

BEHOLD ATRAHASIS'S DAUGHTER!

BEHOLD YOUR RIGHTFUL QUEEN -- WHO SHALL LEAD YOU TO VICTORY AGAINST YOUR CONQUERORS!

SHEMITES! HYR-KANIANS! UNITE AGAINST THE STYGIANS AND THEIR KUSHITE ALLIES!

FORWARD -- FOR ASGALUN!

IN THE FOREFRONT OF THE CROWD, SEVERAL ASGALUNIM HAVE HIDDEN SWORDS AGAINST SUCH A MOMENT -- AND NOW THEY DRAW THEM--

DEATH TO STYGIAN DOGS!

YET, MANY IN THE MILLING THRONG HANG BACK -- FEARFUL -- TO SEE THEIR COUNTRYMEN GUTTED BY SPEARS MADE IN KHEMI AND LUXUR...

AND THEY WOULD DOUBTLESS DISPERSE NOW IN ABJECT FRIGHT -- CARING MORE FOR LIFE THAN LIBERTY--

-- BUT THAT M'GORA AND THE DISGUISED CORSAIRS, FROM THE KUSHITE RANKS, THROW SPEARS OF THEIR OWN!

YASUNGA! LARANGA! NOW!

-- INTO THE LINES OF THE HYRKANIANS!

TREACHERY! THE STYGIANS MUST HAVE ORDERED THE KUSHITES TO LOOSE THEIR SPEARS ON US!

LET US CAST OUR LOTS, THEN, WITH THE SHEMITES!

IT IS OUR ONLY CHANCE!

A MOMENT LATER, THOUGH BÊLIT HERSELF IS DOUBTLESS FORGOTTEN IN THE FRAY, THE BATTLE IS JOINED--

--A ROUGH-HEWN, SUDDEN ALLIANCE OF SHEMITES AND HYRKANIANS AGAINST STYGIANS AND KUSHITES!

THE SHEER NUMBER OF SHEMITES, ADDED TO THE HYRKANIAN SWORDS, MORE THAN COMPENSATES FOR THE BETTER ARMS OF THEIR FOEMEN...

...AND, WITHIN SECONDS, THE GREAT SQUARE RUNS RED WITH BLOOD...

..., WHILE, TOWERING OVER ALL, THE STONE LIONS BEFORE THE PALACE LOOK DOWN UPON A SCENE OF CARNAGE IN THE NAME OF KINGSHIP.

IT IS NEITHER THE FIRST NOR THE LAST SLAUGHTER TO BE CARRIED OUT IN THE NAME OF A ROYAL LINEAGE.

THE HANDFUL OF CONFUSED STYGIANS ATOP THE PALACE STEPS FALL, IN A FEW FRENZIED INSTANTS, BEFORE THE SLASHING, SLAYING SWORD OF CONAN THE CIMMERIAN--

--WHO IS THANKFUL THE CROWD DOES NOT KNOW THAT HE IS LIKEWISE THE HATED AMRA, PIRATE OF THE SEAS--

--OR THAT THIS BÊLIT IS THE SAME ONE WHO RAVAGES ALL SHIPPING, EVEN THAT OF SHEM!

ZULA! STRAY NOT FAR FROM BÊLIT'S SIDE!

THE STYGIANS WOULD GIVE MUCH TO SEE HER DIE!

IT'S HARD TO GUARD THE LADY, FRIEND CONAN--

--WHEN **SHE'S** AS BUSY SLAYING STYGIANS AS **YOU AND I!**

WOMAN! IN CROM'S NAME-- **KEEP OUT OF HARM'S WAY!**

AND LET **YOU** AND ALL THE OTHERS DO ALL THE FIGHTING **FOR ME?!**

NOT LIKELY!

WHILE **ONE** STYGIAN LIVES, BELIT SHALL FIGHT IN THE **FOREFRONT** OF BATTLE!

THEN THERE'S NOTHING TO **DO** FOR IT, I GUESS...

-- BUT SEE TO IT THERE ARE **NO** STYGIANS LEFT HERE TO **CONFRONT** YOU!

AND, WITHIN MOMENTS-- THERE ARE **NOT!**

THUS, SINCE NO **ARROWS** ARE LIKELY TO BE FIRED FROM THE SHOUTING, BLOOD-CRAZED THRONG BELOW, THE SHE-PIRATE QUEEN STANDS BENEATH THE GREAT CARVED HEAD OF A STONE KING OF BEASTS--

--TO **SURVEY** THE CARNAGE BEING CARRIED OUT BELOW IN **HER NAME**--

--NOT REALIZING THAT AN EVEN **DEADLIER** DANGER LURKS AT HER VERY **BACK**--!

THIS IS MY ONE CHANCE TO **KILL** HER--AND **REGAIN** THE THRONE, WHEN THE LAST **STYGIAN** IS DEAD!

THAT SHE SHOULD STAND SO **CLOSE** TO THE VERY **HIDING-PLACE** I'VE CHOSEN!

NO, MY KING! THIS MAD PLAN OF YOURS **WILL NOT WORK!**

IF YOU **SHOW** YOUR-SELF, YOU ARE A **DEAD MAN!**

"AND YOU ARE *ALREADY* ONE--FOR *OPPOSING* THE WILL OF YOUR *KING!*"

"*VENGEANCE* MUST AND SHALL BE *MINE!*"

URRKK--!

IT IS PROBABLE THAT *BÊLIT,* TOO, IS THINKING OF REVENGE AS SHE STANDS BEFORE THE LION-IMAGE...

...*A REVENGE THWARTED,* AS LONG AS *NIM-KARRAK* IS NOT FOUND...

IN THE MELEE, SHE DOES NOT REALIZE... THAT *HE* HAS FOUND *HER!*

FORTUNATELY, ANOTHER PAIR OF EYES IS DIVERTED IN TIME--

BÊLIT-- BEHIND YOU--!

AND, IF *SHE* CANNOT HEAR ABOVE THE TUMULT--

--STILL, THE ROYAL ASSASSIN'S UPRAISED DAGGER-HAND CAN BE *STAYED*--

-- BY THE HYPNOTIC *GLANCE* OF THE DESPERATE *ZULA,* WHO MANAGES FOR A SPLIT-SECOND TO CATCH THE USURPER'S *GAZE*--

--LONG ENOUGH FOR *REALITY* TO BE OVER-TURNED IN NIM-KARRAK'S EYES --

--SO THAT A *CARNIVORE OF STONE* SUDDENLY SEEMS TO *LIVE*-- *MOVE*-- EVEN *MORE!*

NNOOO!!

THE *DEPOSED KING* STUMBLES *BACK-WARD*--

--NOT RECALLING UNTIL *TOO LATE* THAT HE WAS ON THE *EDGE* OF A PLATFORM, HIGH ABOVE THE BLOOD-CRAZED CROWD!

AAAAAAAA

LIKE A DISCARDED *PLAYTHING* HE FALLS, HEADFIRST--

AND, FROM HIS *TWISTED ASPECT* MOMENTS LATER AT THE *FOOT* OF THE *STAIRS,* IT IS OBVIOUS TO *ANY WHO LOOK*--

--THAT THE SHE-PIRATE HAS BEEN *CHEATED* OF HER *LONG-SOUGHT VENGEANCE!*

NO! IT *CAN'T* BE!

I WON'T LET IT--!

BUT IT *IS,* OF COURSE.

WHILE, HIGH ABOVE, A *RAVEN* CASTS A *SARDONIC* EYE AT THE *ONE-SIDED* BATTLE BELOW...

... AND FLIES OFF *SOUTH-EASTWARD.*

AFTER ALL, WITH PTOR-NUBIS *DEAD,* THOTH-*AMON* AND KING CTESPHON MUST KEEP IN TOUCH *SOMEHOW* WITH EVENTS IN ASGALUN--EVEN *UNWISHED-FOR* ONES.

AND *ONE-SIDED* THE BATTLE MOST DEFINITELY IS--

--AS THE SHEMITES AND HYRKANIANS LOSE THEIR *FEAR* OF THE STYGIANS-- THE ONE THING WHICH HAS HELD THEM IN *CHECK.*

IMBALAYO, STRIVING *BELATEDLY* TO REGAIN CONTROL OF HIS MEN, HAS BEEN OF A MIND TO *KEEP* HIS AGREEMENTS WITH THE *BELEAGUERED* STYGIANS.

BUT, WHEN HE SEES THAT AFFAIRS ARE *HOPELESS* IN THAT DIRECTION--

--HE ORDERS HIS KUSHITES TO *CEASE* FIGHTING HYRKANIANS AND SHEMITES--

--AND TO TURN UPON THE *FEW* REMAINING STYGIANS INSTEAD!

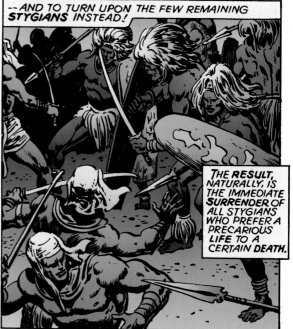

THE *RESULT,* NATURALLY, IS THE *IMMEDIATE SURRENDER* OF ALL STYGIANS WHO PREFER A *PRECARIOUS LIFE* TO A *CERTAIN DEATH.*

THEN, DURING THE INEVITABLE *LULL* AS THE HOSTILITIES WIND DOWN...

MEN OF ASGALUN!

HEAR THE WORDS OF YOUR QUEEN!

NOT ONLY SHEMITES, BUT ALSO THE *MERCENARIES*, LOOK UP AS THOSE REGAL TONES ROLL ACROSS THE GREAT SQUARE...

KNOW YOU THAT NIM-KARRAK THE USURPER IS DEAD--A VICTIM OF HIS OWN SCHEMING!

I, THE DAUGHTER OF ATRAHASIS, AM NOW THE RESTORED SOVEREIGN OF PELISHTIA AND THIS CITY!

HOW DO WE KNOW YOU ARE ATRAHASIS'S DAUGHTER--WHO WAS LONG THOUGHT DEAD?

YOU WILL TAKE, I KNOW, THE SWORN WORD OF BAL-YAMM, PRIEST OF ISHTAR--

--AND THERE ARE WAYS THAT I CAN MAKE MY TRUE SELF KNOWN TO HIM!

THEN-- LET THE DAUGHTER OF ATRAHASIS BE QUEEN OF ASGALUN!

AS SHE SHALL!

BÊLIT--YOU'VE EARNED YONDER CROWN, FOR SURE--

BUT, ARE YOU CERTAIN YOU WANT TO BECOME QUEEN OF THIS FICKLE POPULACE?

CROM, BUT THEY SEEM AS LIKELY TO TURN ON YOU AT ANY MOMENT AS THEY DID ON THE STYGIANS-- AND THEY HAVE ALL THE BACKBONE OF A SQUID FROM THE WESTERN SEA!

I WANT THE CROWN-- SO I'LL TAKE IT, MY LOVER.

IF I CHANGE MY MIND, I CAN ALWAYS TAKE IT OFF AGAIN!

NAY, DAUGHTER OF ATRAHASIS--

WHAT SAY YOU, BAL-YAMM?

I'VE LITTLE DOUBT THAT I CAN ESTABLISH YOU AS WHO YOU ARE-- BUT YOU ARE IGNORANT OF THE TRADITIONS OF THIS LAND YOU LEFT SO LONG AGO.

THE CROWN OF PELISHTIA, ONCE DONNED, CAN BE RENOUNCED NEVER--

--AND ONLY DEATH CAN FREE YOU FROM IT!

IF YOU WERE TO ABDICATE AT SOME FUTURE TIME, THE MOB WOULD SLAY YOU.

IT HAS HAPPENED BEFORE.

AT THE PRIEST'S WORDS, THE SHE-CORSAIR STARES AT THE CROWN...

...AND IT SEEMS FAR HEAVIER THAN A MOMENT BEFORE.

TO BE QUEEN BY **CHOICE** IS ONE THING -- BUT, TO BE QUEEN FOR **FEAR** OF YOUR LIFE -- !

NO, COUSIN -- CALL **ME** NOT "**MAJESTY**," BUT RATHER **YOURSELF**!

YOUR **DESIRES**, HIGHNESS, NO LONGER MAKE ANY **DIFFERENCE** --

THEN, ABRUPTLY, SHE SPOTS THE SOLUTION TO THE GRONDARIAN KNOT THAT CONFRONTS HER...

URIAZ!

M-MAJESTY...?

MEN OF ASGALUN -- BEHOLD YOUR **KING**!

N-NO!! I -- I NEVER **WANTED** --

YOU ARE **RIGHTFUL KING** NOW IN PELISHTIA --

-- UNTIL THE **HOUR** OF YOUR **DEATH**!

BUT -- ALL I EVER **DESIRED** -- WAS MY **PLEASURE GARDENS**...!

I THINK YOU'VE MADE A **WISE MOVE**, BÊLIT -- FOR **YOURSELF**, IF NOT NECESSARILY FOR **ASGALUN**.

AYE, WOMAN! IT WAS ALWAYS CLEAR TO ME THAT IT WAS THE **REVENGE** ON **NIM-KARRAK** YOU WANTED -- **NOT** THE THRONE ITSELF!

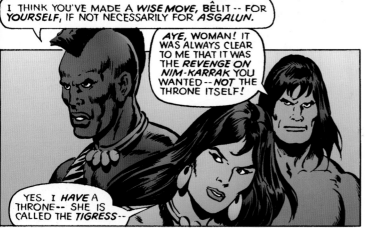

YES. I **HAVE** A THRONE -- SHE IS CALLED THE **TIGRESS** --

-- AND SHE WAITS NOW AT **ANCHOR**, MANY LEAGUES FROM HERE.

COME! THIS SECRET PASSAGE WILL TAKE US **OUT** OF THE CITY --

-- BEFORE THE PEOPLE LEARN THEY NEARLY CROWNED A HATED **SHE-PIRATE** QUEEN OF THEIR PROVINCE!

THEY'D HAVE NO LOVE FOR **AMRA** EITHER, I FEAR.

AS IT TURNS OUT, THE MENFOLK OF ASGALUN HAVE LITTLE LOVE FOR **ANYONE**...

FOOL! I SAY **AKHÎROM**, WHEREVER HE IS, WOULD MAKE A BETTER KING THAN FAT **URIAZ**!

AKHÎROM -- OR A **DONKEY**, FOR THAT MATTER!

SILENCE, DOG! YOU SPEAK OF YOUR **KING**!

AND WHERE WERE **YOU** WHEN THE REST OF US WERE RISKING OUR LIVES FOR **ASGALUN**, eh?

ONE THING LEADS TO ANOTHER, AND ERE LONG--

--EACH FACTION IS AT THE OTHER'S THROAT--

--SAVE FOR THE *STYGIANS*, WHO ARE FEW ENOUGH TO *KNOW* WHEN THEY ARE *DEFEATED*.

WHILE, FROM *LIBUN HILLS* BEYOND THE GATES..

ALREADY THE *SOUNDS* OF *STRIFE* ECHO FROM THE CITY!

I'VE HAD A *NARROW ESCAPE*, IT SEEMS.

NARROWER EVEN THAN YOU *THINK*, PERHAPS.

LOOK THERE--APPROACHING FROM THE *NORTHEAST*--!

"I NEED NO *MAGIC GLASS* TO KNOW THAT IS THE ARMY OF *AKHÎROM*, THE ONLY OTHER MAN WITH A CLAIM TO ASGALUN'S CROWDED THRONE!

"HE'S RUMORED TO BE *QUITE MAD*, OF COURSE -- BUT SINCE WHEN DID *THAT* EVER STOP ANYONE FROM BECOMING A *LEADER OF MEN?*"

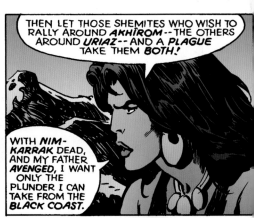

THEN LET THOSE SHEMITES WHO WISH TO RALLY AROUND *AKHÎROM* -- THE OTHERS AROUND *URIAZ* -- AND A *PLAGUE* TAKE THEM *BOTH!*

WITH *NIM-KARRAK* DEAD, AND MY FATHER *AVENGED*, I WANT ONLY THE PLUNDER I CAN TAKE FROM THE *BLACK COAST.*

REVENGE *ISN'T* SO SWEET AS IT'S *WHISPERED* TO BE, IS IT, BÊLIT?

I SLEW *PTOR-NUBIS*, BUT I DON'T FEEL MUCH *BETTER* FOR IT.

GOOD! IF I NEVER AGAIN *SET FOOT* ON STYGIAN SOIL, IT WILL BE *TOO SOON.*

PERHAPS I *WON'T* BE TAKING THAT VENGEANCE-TRIP TO *KHESHATTA* AFTER ALL, CONAN.

READY TO *GO*, BÊLIT?

MORE THAN READY, MY LOVER.

WE'VE BEEN *ASHORE* SO LONG...

... I JUST HOPE WE HAVEN'T LOST OUR *SEA-LEGS...!*

NEXT ISSUE: THE BEAST-KING OF ABOMBI!

"Know, O prince, that between the years when the oceans drank Atlantis and the gleaming cities, and the rise of the sons of Aryas, there was an Age undreamed of, when shining kingdoms lay spread across the world like blue mantles beneath the stars.
"Hither came Conan, the Cimmerian, black-haired, sullen-eyed, sword in hand, a thief, a reaver, a slayer, with gigantic melancholies and gigantic mirth, to tread the jeweled thrones of the Earth under his sandaled feet."

—The Nemedian Chronicles.

Stan Lee PRESENTS: CONAN THE BARBARIAN™

BUT WHAT OF YOUR *OWN* DESIRE FOR VENGEANCE-- ON THE *STYGIAN WIZARD* WHO TRIED TO HAVE YOU *SLAIN?*

YOU SAID YOU'RE HEADING *NORTH*-- NOT SOUTH TO HIS HOUSE IN *KHESHATTA!*

BECAUSE I FOUND REVENGE *LESS SATIS-FYING* THAN I'D THOUGHT...

...WHEN I *SLEW PTOR-NUBIS,* WHO HAD FIRST SOLD ME INTO *SLAVERY.*

SUIT *YOURSELF,* ZULA--BUT AS FOR *ME,* I THINK I'LL CONTINUE TO FIND REVENGE SATISFYING WHEN SOMEONE WRONGS ME.

MAYBE IT'S BECAUSE I'M AN *IGNORANT BARBARIAN* FROM THE NORTHLANDS, WHILE YOU EDUCATED YOURSELF IN THE *CITY OF MAGICIANS.*

YOU'RE ABOUT AS IGNORANT AS A *FOX,* FRIEND CONAN.

GODDESS...!

LARANGA, AJAGA, AND THE OTHERS HAVE ASKED ME TO *SPEAK* FOR US *ALL.* WE HOPE YOU UNDERSTAND OUR WISH TO GO *NORTH* WITH THE *ZAMBALLAH...*

I *DO,* YASUNGA.

YOUR DESIRES WERE *FED,* IN FACT, IN *MY* SERVICE-- WHEN YOU SPIED FOR ME IN *ASGALUN,* OF LATE.

THIS IS MY PRAYER-- THAT MY MOTHER, THE *DEATH-GODDESS,* STAY HER PALE HAND FROM *ALL* OF YOU-- AND GRANT YOU *LONG LIVES!*

NOW, *FARE YOU WELL,* ALL!

GIVE MY REGARDS TO THE *FIRST HYPERBOREAN* YOU SEE, ZULA--BY *SLITTING HIS THROAT!*

NOT UNLESS HE DRAWS A KNIFE ON ME *FIRST,* I FEAR.

TILL WE *MEET AGAIN,* ZULA!

CROM'S DEVILS!

ZULA... *ALL* OF THEM...

THEY'VE *VANISHED* --INTO *THIN AIR!*

HAH! LOOK **AGAIN**, BOTH OF YOU! ZULA IS BUT **TEASING** YOU...HE IS **THERE**!

WHAT ARE YOU **TALKING** ABOUT, N'YAGA? I DON'T--

ZULA! TAKE **PITY** ON YOUR OLD FRIENDS, EH?

SUDDENLY, THE CORSAIRS ALL **REAPPEAR**...REMINDING CONAN AND BÊLIT THAT, AFTER ALL, ZULA IS ALSO A **MASTER OF HYPNOSIS**.

GOOD-BYE, CHILDREN!

WHEN THEY VANISH A **SECOND TIME**, IT IS OVER A DISTANT **HORIZON**...

AND, THOUGH SHE SAYS NOTHING, THE **SHE-PIRATE** CASTS A FURTIVE GLANCE AT HER LOVER, OUT OF THE CORNERS OF HER DARK EYES.

CONAN'S FACE IS A GRIM **MASK**, DEVOID OF EMOTION.

SOON, TAKING ADVANTAGE OF THE TIDES, THE **TIGRESS** LEAVES ONCE MORE THE **SHORES OF SHEM**...A BIT **SHORT-HANDED** NOW, YET **PROUDLY** STILL, FOR ALL THAT...

CONAN, BELOVED...HAD **YOU** ANY DESIRE TO GO NORTH **WITH** ZULA?

AFTER ALL, IT'S BEEN **THREE YEARS** SINCE YOU LAST STALKED THE **HYBORIAN LANDS**!

THE DAY I WANT TO **LEAVE**, OR YOU WANT ME TO **GO**...I **SHALL** GO, GIRL.

UNTIL THEN, LET'S HAVE NO MORE TALK OF **ANY** DESIRES OF MINE...

...SAVE THE ONE I FEEL FOR **YOU**!

THE PIRATE SHIP HEADS HER REGAL PROW STRAIGHT OUT TO SEA-- WHERE SHE'LL TURN **SOUTH**, INTO FAMILIAR WATERS. HER DESTINATION: **THE BLACK COAST**...

...WHERE BÊLIT IS **UNCROWNED** QUEEN!

LOOK TO *PORT*, CORSAIRS-- **--WHERE ONCE WAS THE VILLAGE OF THE *MATUBIS*!**

"*WAS*"?! WHAT THE DEVIL DOES HE MEAN BY--?

AMOURS OF ISHTAR!

THERE ARE **NO MORE WORDS** SPOKEN FOR A MOMENT ABOARD THE **TIGRESS**...

FOR, **ASHORE**, WHERE ONLY A FEW MONTHS PAST THERE HAD FLOURISHED A **SIZABLE SEA-VILLAGE** OF A BLACK-COAST TRIBE LOYAL TO BÊLIT, IF ADMITTEDLY LARGELY OF **NECESSITY**...

...THERE IS NOW NOTHING BUT **OLD, CHARRED REMAINS**, NO LONGER EVEN **SMOLDERING**.

NOR DOES ANY SIGN OF **HUMAN LIFE** STIR AMONG THE MONTHS-OLD EMBERS.

AND, MOVING FURTHER SOUTH IN THE DAYS THAT FOLLOW, THE PIRATES FIND THE SAME SCENE **REPEATED** OR EERILY **PARALLELED** SEVERAL TIMES OVER--

MORE **BURNT-OUT** VILLAGES, SOME LARGE, SOME SMALL... AND, IN ONE PLACE, A VILLAGE WITHOUT A SINGLE HUT **DAMAGED**, BUT WITH NO **LIVING THING** WITHIN ITS STILL-INTACT WALLS!

WHAT *HAPPENED* HERE, CONAN--THAT EVERYONE EITHER WAS *KILLED*, OR AT LEAST *FRIGHTENED* INLAND?

WE'LL KNOW THE *ANSWER*, BÊLIT, IF AND WHEN WE FIND SOMEONE WHO *DIDN'T* EITHER FLEE... OR DIE.

WHAT THINK *YOU*, SHAMAN?

I *THINK*, AMRA, THAT WHEN YOU FIND THE *PERPETRATORS* OF THESE DEEDS, YOU HAD BEST BE READY TO USE BOTH SWORDS *AND* WIZARDRY AGAINST THEM! THERE IS SOMETHING... *UNNATURAL* ABOUT ALL THIS.

AND SOUTH, EVER **SOUTHWARD**, CONTINUES THE ERRANT **TIGRESS**...

...TILL AT LAST IT COMES TO THE MOUTH OF THAT PEACEABLE RIVER WHERE DWELL THE FAITHFUL WATAMBI TRIBE. *

WE'LL TAKE ONLY N'YAGA AND A FEW CORSAIRS WITH US, MY LOVER-- LEAVING THE REST TO GUARD THE SHIP.

YOU'RE THE CAPTAIN, LASS.

STRANGE THAT CHIEF OMBASSA ISN'T HERE TO GREET US, AS HE USUALLY DOES.

SURELY HE WOULDN'T DARE ATTACK US IN AMBUSH!

YOU'RE OVERLY SUSPICIOUS, WOMAN. HE WAS GRATEFUL FOR THE HELP WE GAVE HIM LAST TRIP, AGAINST THE RIVER-DRAGONS.

STILL, YOU'RE RIGHT THAT SOMETHING STRANGE HAS HAPPENED...

FOR, THERE'S THE WATAMBI VILLAGE-- AND THERE DOESN'T SEEM TO BE EVEN A LOOK-OUT POSTED!

IN THIS COUNTRY, THAT'S A GOOD WAY FOR A TRIBE TO GET WIPED OUT BY A SURPRISE ATTACK!

HO, WATAMBIS!

HO, OMBASSA!

IS ANYONE THERE?

IT'S BÊLIT AND AMRA WHO CALL-- AND WE COME AS FRIENDS!

THE WATAMBIS HAVE NO FRIENDS, AMRA-- FOR WHAT NEED HAVE GHOSTS OF SUCH?

ENTER, IF YOU WILL-- BUT YOU COME TO A VILLAGE OF THE DEAD.

OMBASSA!

EVEN THE BLACK CORSAIRS BELOW, WHO ARE LESS FAMILIAR WITH THE WATAMBI DIALECT THAN THEIR LEADERS, NOTICE THE LISTLESS TONE OF THE CHIEFTAIN'S VOICE...THE EERIE SLOWNESS OF HIS MOTIONS...

...LIKE THOSE OF A MAN ENTRANCED.

YOU ARE **WELCOME**, ALL-- BUT SADLY, WE HAVE **NO TRIBUTE** FOR YOU, FOR THE SECOND TIME.

IT'S NOT IVORY OR OSTRICH PLUMES WE WANT TODAY, OMBASSA...BUT **ANSWERS**.

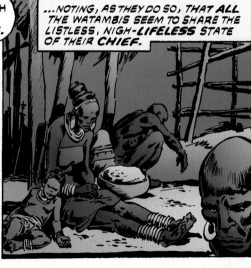

...NOTING, AS THEY DO SO, THAT **ALL** THE WATAMBIS SEEM TO SHARE THE LISTLESS, NIGH-**LIFELESS** STATE OF THEIR **CHIEF**.

THEN **COME**, AND YOU SHALL HAVE THEM...THOUGH THEY'LL NOT BE **HAPPY** ONES FOR YOU.

*SILENTLY, SOMBRELY, THE PIRATES **FOLLOW** THE GAUNT CHIEFTAIN THROUGH THE VILLAGE STREETS...*

IT **IS** LIKE A CITY OF THE DEAD, BY CROM!

WE'LL GET TO THE **BOTTOM** OF THIS! I **VOW** IT--

--BY ALL THE JEWELS IN THE **CROWN I FORESWORE!**

NYAMI--A HOSTAGE? BUT--TAKEN BY **WHOM?**

SINCE WE CLEANED OUT THAT NEST OF **DRAGON-RIDERS**, THIS COUNTRY SHOULD BE REVOLTINGLY **PEACEFUL.**

HAVE YOU EVER HEARD, O AMRA-- O BÊLIT-- OF **ABOMBI?**

ABOMBI?! SOME PILE OF DESERTED **RUINS**, ISN'T IT? WE'VE SAILED PAST IT ON OCCASION, **SOUTH** OF HERE!

*CONAN, BÊLIT AND N'YAGA JOIN OMBASSA AND HIS **WITCH DOCTOR** INSIDE...*

NOW, WHAT HAS BE-FALLEN YOUR PEOPLE, OLD FRIEND?

WE HAVE BECOME A **SUBJECT RACE**, O GODDESS--MY **OWN DAUGHTER** HELD A **HOSTAGE** AGAINST OUR LOYALTY TO A **NEW** AND DREADED MASTER!

"**AYE**," OMBASSA CONTINUES, "**DESERTED** ONCE, CERTAINLY--BUT **NOT** RUINS! THE CITY WAS ABANDONED AT ITS **HEIGHT**, EONS AGO, BY MEN OF SOME UNKNOWN **ELDER RACE.**

"FOR LONG CENTURIES, ONLY THE **WAVES** HAVE DARED TRY TO ASSAIL ABOMBI'S IMPREGNABLE YET UNMANNED **RAMPARTS.**

"MOONS AGO, AN *INLAND CHIEF* CAST HIS *OWN SON* OUT OF HIS TRIBE, AFTER THE UNGRATEFUL ONE TRIED TO *OUST* HIS OWN FATHER FROM POWER.

"HIS NAME WAS *AJAGA*... AND HE WAS A *MIGHTY WARRIOR.*

"WITH A HANDFUL OF SPEARMEN *LOYAL* TO HIM, THE SON WENT INTO THE *WILDERNESS,* EITHER TO FIND A NEW HOME... OR TO *PERISH.*

"RATHER THAN STRIKE OUT STILL FURTHER *INLAND,* AJAGA LED HIS FOLLOWERS TO *ABOMBI.*

"SEEING THOSE STILL-STANDING *WALLS* WHICH NO MAN CAN SMASH, AJAGA DECLARED HIM-SELF *KING* OF THE CITY-- AND DESTINED TO *REVIVE* ITS FORGOTTEN GLORIES.

"HIS *FELLOW EXILES,* HOWEVER, WOULD NOT FOLLOW HIM *INTO* THE CITY... FOR, ITS LEGEND MAKES IT BOTH *HOLY* AND *HAUNTED* TO ALL WHO HAVE HEARD OF IT.

"THUS, AJAGA CLIMBED *ALONE* TO THE TOP OF THE *HIGHEST PEAK* OVERLOOKING ABOMBI, WHILE HIS MEN EXPECTED HIM AT ANY MOMENT TO BE KILLED BY *LIGHTNING* FROM ON HIGH...

"...AND HE *PRAYED,* IN PLAIN SIGHT OF THE FRIGHTENED ONES BELOW, TO HOVERING *SPIRITS...*

"SUDDENLY, THE WATCHERS SAW THAT WHICH *NO MAN LIVING* HAD EVER SEEN *BEFORE...*

"...AS A *THICK MIST* CAME UP OUT OF NOWHERE, TO FORM A SHIFTING *MASK* AROUND THE PRAYING EXILE...

"...A MASK THAT CAME TO BE SHAPED LIKE A *PANTHER'S HEAD!*

"WHEN THE MIST *VANISHED* AS SWIFTLY AS IT HAD COME, AJAGA LAY *UNCONSCIOUS* ON THE ROCKS HIGH ABOVE.

"HE SHOWED NO SIGN OF *LIFE...*

"...NOT EVEN WHEN HIS FOLLOWERS LOWERED HIM FROM THE PEAK.

"YET, HOURS LATER, A POISONOUS *SERPENT* CRAWLED UPON HIS UNMOVING, *UNBREATHING* FORM... AND HE SUDDENLY *DREW BREATH* ONCE MORE!

"*MORE*-- HE GREETED THE DEADLY VIPER AS IF IT WERE A LONG-LOST *BROTHER!*

HOW DID YOU *LEARN* ALL THIS, OMBASSA?

FROM ONE WHO CAME TO *FEAR* AJAGA IN TIME, AND *FLED* HIS COMPANY, GODDESS.

FOR, AJAGA'S *RETURN TO LIFE* WAS BUT THE *BEGINNING* OF THE MAN'S *DEVILTRY...*

"FROM THAT DAY FORTH, THE *BEASTS OF THE JUNGLE* DID HIS BIDDING...AND *AMBITIOUS MEN*, THWARTED WITHIN THEIR OWN TRIBES, FLOCKED TO HIS STRANGE AND NAMELESS *RITUALS*."

"MOST *VILLAINOUS* OF ALL THESE, IT'S SAID, ARE *TWO BROTHERS*, WHO ARE SAID TO HAVE *SLAIN* THEIR OWN FATHER."

"AS TRIBE AFTER TRIBE *PAID HOMAGE* TO AJAGA, OR ELSE WAS *DRIVEN INLAND*, I RELUCTANTLY PREPARED FOR *WAR*."

"AND, BEFORE LONG, THE DAY *CAME*..."

"...WHEN THE *BEAST-KING OF ABOMBI* STOOD OUTSIDE THE GATES OF *OUR* VILLAGE..."

CHIEF OF THE WATAMBIS! GIVE US *TRIBUTE*--AND YOUR *DAUGHTER* AS HOSTAGE-- OR FACE THE *WRATH OF AJAGA!*

"THE SPOTTED *LEOPARD* AT HIS SIDE TOLD ME THE WHISPERS ALL WERE *TRUE*."

WE PAY *NO ONE* TRIBUTE, INTRUDER...

...NO ONE BUT *BÊLIT*, WHO *PROTECTS* US IN TURN FROM OTHER TRIBES!

"IT *SADDENS* ME, GODDESS, TO REPORT HIS *ANSWER*--"

BÊLIT!? ⸮*FAUGHH!*⸮ WHEN DID THAT PALE-SKINNED WITCH DO *ANYTHING* FOR YOU? SHE IS *FAR AWAY* SOMEWHERE-- PERHAPS *DEAD*.

AJAGA IS *HERE*-- NOW!

GIVE IN TO MY DEMANDS -- OR SUFFER!

"MY RESPONSE WAS *RASH*, PERHAPS.

"AJAGA HAD NOT COME UNDER A *SIGN OF TRUCE*, SO I RAISED MY WAR-SPEAR AND AIMED FOR HIS EVIL *HEART*..."

"YET, SOME *SPIRIT* DIVERTED MY AIM SO THAT I MERELY SLEW HIS INHUMAN *FAMILIAR*, INSTEAD...

RRARG

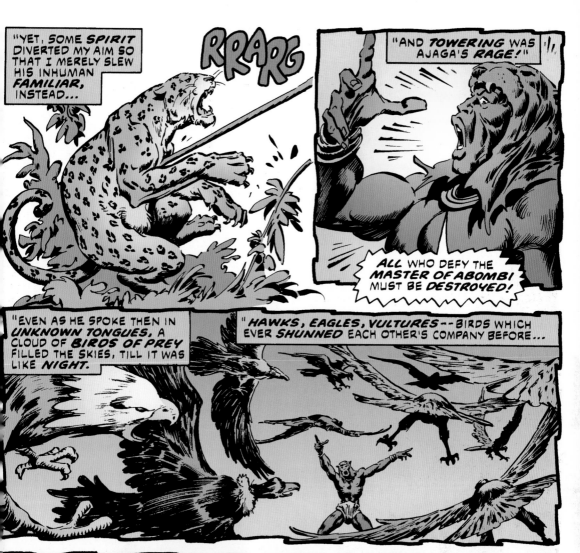

"AND *TOWERING* WAS AJAGA'S *RAGE!*"

ALL WHO DEFY THE *MASTER OF ABOMBI* MUST BE *DESTROYED!*

"EVEN AS HE SPOKE THEN IN *UNKNOWN TONGUES*, A CLOUD OF *BIRDS OF PREY* FILLED THE SKIES, TILL IT WAS LIKE *NIGHT*.

"HAWKS, EAGLES, VULTURES -- BIRDS WHICH EVER *SHUNNED* EACH OTHER'S COMPANY BEFORE...

"...NOW ATTACKED IN A BLINDING, DEADLY *MASS*...

"...AND GREAT WAS OUR *LOSS* BEFORE THE MOCKING AJAGA CALLED THEM *AWAY*.

"IN OUR WATCHFUL FOOLISHNESS, WE THOUGHT HIM *BEATEN*, AT GREAT COST -- AND LOOKED MAINLY TO THE *SKY* THAT NIGHT.

"BUT IT WAS *CRAWLING* THAT THE NEXT THREAT CAME...

"...BOTH *VENOMOUS* SNAKES, AND THOSE THAT *CRUSH THE BONES*.

"AND ANY FALSE *JOY* I MAY HAVE FELT IN KILLING AJAGA'S *LEOPARD* SWIFTLY VANISHED...

"...WHEN ANOTHER, EVEN *LARGER* ONE DARED APPROACH OUR VILLAGE, AS *NONE* HAD EVER DONE BEFORE...

"...TO *SLAY* MORE THAN ONE MAN, BEFORE FLEEING AGAIN TO ITS MASTER'S SIDE.

"THERE BE THOSE, IN FACT, WHO SAY IT WAS *AJAGA* HIMSELF WHO STRUCK THUS...

"FOR, ALL MEN KNOW THAT *SOME* MEN CAN TURN THEMSELVES INTO *BEASTS* AT WILL!

"STILL, WE *REFUSED* TO BEND THE KNEE, THOUGH WITH FALTERING HEARTS.

"BUT, LATER THAT SAME NIGHT, *HULKING SHADOWS* KILLED TWO BRAVE WARRIORS WHO GUARDED THE HUT OF MY DAUGHTER *NYAMI!*...

"...AND CARRIED HER OFF, AS IF SHE HAD BEEN A *SACK OF WHEAT.*

"*BABOONS* THEY WERE --THOUGH *LARGER* THAN MOST...

"...AND *FAR* FROM THEIR NATIVE HAUNTS IN THE *HIGH, ROCKY PLACES.*

"*SCREAMING* AND *FIGHTING,* MY DAUGHTER WAS TAKEN FROM UNDER THE VERY *NOSES* OF HER PEOPLE!

"AND, THOUGH IT WAS *MY OWN SPEAR* WHICH SLEW ONE OF THE HIDEOUS *MINIONS OF AJAGA...*

"...IT DID NOT BRING HER *BACK* TO ME!

"SOON I HEARD THE VOICE OF *AJAGA...*"

NOW, CHIEF OF THE WATAM- BI--

WILL YOU *PAY TRIBUTE* TO ME--

--OR SHALL THIS, MY *FURRY BROTHER,* TEAR HER LIMB FROM LIMB *BEFORE YOUR EYES?*

"I AM A *CHIEFTAIN* AS WELL AS A *FATHER,* GODDESS...AMRA. I WOULD HAVE LET MY OWN DAUGHTER *PERISH,* RATHER THAN BETRAY MY TRUST.

"BUT, *MY PEOPLE,* TOO, KNEW...

"...THAT WE COULD NOT FIGHT FOREVER AGAINST THE *WHOLE JUNGLE.*

"THUS, WE *PARLEYED* WITH THE MASTER OF ABOMBI, AND GAVE HIM THE *TRIBUTE* WE HAD SET ASIDE AGAINST THE DAY OF *YOUR* RETURN."

WE WILL *KEEP* OUR WORD, AJAGA, AND NOT *FIGHT* AGAINST YOU.

NOW, YOU MUST *RETURN* MY DAUGHTER!

NO!

SHE WILL REMAIN WITH ME IN *ABOMBI,* AS A HOSTAGE--AND AS ONE OF MY *BRIDES,* SUCH AS *EACH CONQUERED TRIBE* HAS GIVEN ME.

I SHALL FOUND A *NEW* TRIBE-- RULED BY THE *DYNASTY OF AJAGA!*

THUS *ENDS* MY STORY-- BUT *NOT* MY TRIBE'S *SHAME*.

THE *MIST* YOU SPOKE OF, CHIEFTAIN-- HAVE YOU ANY IDEA *HOW* IT GAVE AJAGA *POWER OVER ANIMALS?*

YOU ARE A *TORMENTED* MAN, OMBASSA. I'M SORRY I WAS *HARSH* WITH YOU.

MY *WITCH-MAN* SAYS THAT HE DOES, AMRA.

ONE *NAME* ONLY COMES TO ME IN MY *JUJU TRANCE...*

...THE NAME OF *JHEBBAL SAG!*

JHEBBAL SAG? WHO IS *THAT?*

HE WAS A *MIGHTY BEING* WHO ONCE WAS *WORSHIPED* BY ALL MEN... AND ALL *BEASTS*. THAT WAS IN THE LONG-AGO DAY WHEN MEN *AND* BEASTS SPOKE THE *SAME TONGUE*.

AYE, AMRA... YOU WILL *STILL* FIND MEN, EVEN IN THE BACKWARD PARTS OF CIVILIZED AQUILONIA AND NEMEDIA, WHO HAVE *HEARD* THE NAME.

TODAY, MEN HAVE LARGELY *FORGOTTEN* HIM... MEN, AND *MOST* ANIMALS.

BUT, *SOME* BEASTS STILL *REMEMBER...*

AND THOSE WHO REMEMBER *...OBEY!*

SOMEHOW, *AJAGA* LEARNED JHEBBAL SAG'S *SECRET TONGUE* IN HIS MIST-ENSHROUDED TRANCE!

AND IF AJAGA *DIES*, THE BEASTS WILL NO LONGER *MENACE* THE TRIBES?

AYE, AND HIS OWN UNNATURAL TRIBE WILL *DISPERSE*, LEADERLESS.

THEN N'YAGA WILL RETURN TO THE *TIGRESS*, WHILE WE OTHERS *SEEK OUT* AND *SLAY* THIS AJAGA!

IT WILL NOT BE *EASY*, O AMRA.

NOTHING *IS* THESE DAYS, IT SEEMS.

MY HEART IS *HEAVY*, WITCH-MAN, THAT I CANNOT GO *WITH* THEM. MY *DAUGHTER*--!

YOU GAVE AJAGA THE *WORD OF A CHIEFTAIN*.

DO NOT FEAR, OMBASSA-- THEY *UNDERSTAND*.

THROUGH TRACKLESS JUNGLES GO THE *CORSAIRS*, FOLLOWING A STREAM WHICH WILL TAKE THEM TO *ABOMBI*...

WE *MUST* DEFEAT AJAGA, MY *LOVER*--IF WE'RE TO *REGAIN* OUR POSITION ON THE *BLACK COAST*.

I DIDN'T GIVE UP *ONE* THRONE, ONLY TO SUR-RENDER ANOTHER TO A *MADMAN*!

TRUE--STILL, I'LL CONFESS I PREFER *SAILING CRIMSON SEAS* TO FIGHTING OFF *MOSQUITOS*, DAMN THEM!

N'YAGA'S *POTIONS* WILL GIVE US IMMUNITY TO THEM.

WE MUST *DEFEAT* AJAGA, BEFORE HIS POWER GROWS *TOO STRONG* TO CHAL-LENGE!

THEN, SEVERAL DAYS LATER--

THERE THEY ARE-- THE *BACKSIDE* OF THE PEAKS ON WHICH *ABOMBI* IS BUILT!

SMALL WONDER THEY'RE *NOT* GUARDED!

WE *HOPE*!

THEY'D BE *HARD* TO CLIMB, AYE, FOR *MOST* MEN--

--BUT *NOT* A TRUE SCION OF *CIMMERIA*!

NO *LONE HEROICS* NOW--!

JUST SEARCH-ING FOR *HANDHOLDS* --WHICH ARE FEW AND FAR BETWEEN!

I'LL GO ON *AHEAD*, AND YOU CAN FOLLOW ON THE *ROPE*.

CONAN HAS SPENT SOME HOURS *TEACHING* BÊLIT AND HER MEN THE WAYS OF A *CIMMERIAN HILLMAN*.

ELSE, HE WOULD NEVER DARE TRY TO ASCEND SO SHEER A CLIFF AT *NIGHT*.

YET, THIS EVENING, *SURPRISE* IS OF THE UTMOST IMPORTANCE...

55

--BUT, ALAS, *IMPOSSIBLE* OF ACHIEVEMENT!

CHRR CHRRR

BABOONS!

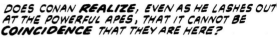

DOES CONAN *REALIZE*, EVEN AS HE LASHES OUT AT THE POWERFUL APES, THAT IT CANNOT BE *COINCIDENCE* THAT THEY ARE HERE?

DOES HE SUDDENLY *SENSE*, PERHAPS, THE SHEER *HOPELESSNESS* OF THE CORSAIRS' MISSION?

IF SO, HE SAYS *NOTHING*--

-- MERELY *STRIKES BACK* WITH HIS SHARP *BLADE*--

--TO GIVE HIS COM-RADES AND THE WOMAN HE LOVES A CHANCE TO *LIVE!*

CHRK

WE'RE *COMING,* CONAN!

ONE DARK PIRATE IS HURLED TO *CERTAIN DEATH*--

AAAAA

--EVEN AS CONAN'S SWORD RISES AND FALLS LIKE A *BUTCHER'S CLEAVER!*

LIKE AN ANIMAL *HIMSELF* IS HE, IN HIS NIGH-BESTIAL *FURY!*

NOR DOES THAT FURY GO *UNADMIRED*--!

HAH! EASY, MY MOTTLED FRIEND!

LOOK, YOU BROTHERS-- KRATO--BEEYA--! *THESE* ARE THE ONES WHO SOUGHT TO BREAK THE *YOKE OF AJAGA!*

CALL OFF YOUR *MONKEYS,* DEVIL--FOR JUST *ONE* MINUTE--

--AND WE'D SOON LEARN *WHOSE* NECK--COULD BEAR THE *MOST* STRAIN--!

WITH A SUPERHUMAN EFFORT, CONAN *FLINGS* HIMSELF AT THE LEERING *BEAST-KING*--

-- ONLY TO HAVE *TWO* OF THE FIERCE *BABOONS* LEAP UPON HIM--

--THEIR MOMENTUM CARRYING THE *THREE* OF THEM OVER THE SIDE OF THE CLIFF --

--AND INTO THE *NIGHT-BLACKENED* FOREST SO VERY FAR BELOW!

CONAN!

UNNG

CORSAIRS! YOUR QUEEN IS DOWN, AND WILL BE *TORN APART* UNLESS YOU *DROP YOUR SPEARS!*

WELL?

FOR THE MEN OF THE SOUTHERN ISLES, IT IS *NO CHOICE* AT ALL.

WEAPONS CAST ASIDE, THEY ARE *HERDED AWAY* BY SEVERAL BABOONS...

...WHILE *BÊLIT,* UNCONSCIOUS, FOLLOWS AFTER.

AND SOMEWHERE, OFF IN THE JUNGLE, A *LION* ROARS...!

NEXT ISSUE: BRIDE OF THE BEAST-KING!

"Know, O prince, that between the years when the oceans drank Atlantis and the gleaming cities, and the rise of the sons of Aryas, there was an Age undreamed of, when shining kingdoms lay spread across the world like blue mantles beneath the stars.

"Hither came Conan, the Cimmerian, black-haired, sullen-eyed, sword in hand, a thief, a reaver, a slayer, with gigantic melancholies and gigantic mirth, to tread the jeweled thrones of the Earth under his sandaled feet."

—The Nemedian Chronicles.

STAN LEE PRESENTS: CONAN THE BARBARIAN™

THE RETURN OF AMRA!

THE STORY SO FAR:
The she-pirate BÊLIT AND SEVERAL OF HER BLACK CORSAIRS HAVE BEEN CAPTURED-- NOT BY HUMAN FORCE ALONE, BUT BY THE POWERFUL SINEWS OF GREAT BABOONS, WHICH OBEY THE SNARLED COMMANDS OF THE ONE CALLED THE BEAST-KING OF ABOMBI...!

GO, HAIRY ONES! TAKE HER TO THE CLIFF-CITY!

THERE, LET HER JOIN MY OTHER HOSTAGE BRIDES--

--THAT ALL THE JUNGLE MAY KNOW AND FEAR THE POWER OF AJAGA, RIGHTFUL HEIR TO THE MANTLE OF JHEBBAL SAG!

ROY THOMAS
WRITER & EDITOR

JOHN BUSCEMA & ERNIE CHAN
ILLUSTRATORS & INNOVATORS

JOE ROSEN LETTERER

JIM SHOOTER CONSULTING EDITOR

FEATURING CHARACTERS AND CONCEPTS CREATED BY
ROBERT E. HOWARD

LG 292

IT IS GOOD, O MASTER OF BEASTS, THAT YOU HAVE CAPTURED THE WHITE SHE-DEMON.

WAS HE A BIRD, THAT HE TOOK WING AND FLEW?

HE IS DEAD; FORGET HIM.

BUT-- WHAT OF HER BRONZED MATE, WHO PLUNGED OVER THE CLIFF?

MOST LIKELY, GREAT ONE...

STILL, THE FOREST BELOW IS THICK, VERY THICK-- AND MY BROTHER AND I WILL NOT REST UNTIL WE SEE HIS MANGLED AND BROKEN BODY... AYE, BEEYA?

KRATO SPEAKS FOR US BOTH, O AJAGA.

THEN LET THE BOTH OF YOU KEEP SILENCE!

YOU ARE MY CHIEFS-- BUT I AM KING OF ABOMBI!

AND I SAY THAT A MAN DOES NOT FALL HUNDREDS OF FEET-- WITHOUT PLUNGING DEAD INTO THE WORLD OF SPIRITS.

NOW COME! WE DEPART FOR MY CITY!

RRRR

BUT, THOUGH AJAGA MAY DICTATE THE ACTIONS OF THE TWO CHIEFTAIN BROTHERS...

...EVEN HE CANNOT KNOW FOR CERTAIN WHAT TRULY HAPPENED, ONLY A FEW MINUTES AGONE...

...WHEN A FIGHTING-MAD CONAN AND TWO SNARLING BABOONS FELL, IN A SINGLE WRITHING MASS, OVER THE CLIFF.

OWN, SICKEN-IGLY DOWN-ARD THEY LUMMETED-- LL THOUGHTS F BATTLE ORGOTTEN OW IN THEIR HEER PANIC.

THE FIRST OF THE SCREECHING APES WAS TORN FROM THE MASS WHEN ALL THREE STRUCK THE HIGHEST BRANCHES OF THE WALL OF TREES FAR BELOW...

...BRANCHES WHICH SLOWED THE HEAD-LONG FALL OF THE OTHER TWO FIGURES... EVER SO SLIGHTLY.

THE TREES ARE MANY-LIMBED AND **TALL** HERE-- TALLER THAN TREES **WILL** BE, WHEN MEN BEGIN TO WRITE WHAT THEY WILL CALL **HISTORY**--

--AND **EACH** LIMB **SLOWED** MORE, EVEN AS IT **BRUISED**--

CHREE

--TILL **BARBARIAN** AND **BABOON** STRUCK THE YIELDING GROUND IN A MARSHY, SOFT-EARTHED PLACE--

--THE **APE** BREAKING, AT THE LAST, THE FALL OF THE **MAN!**

FOR SOME MOMENTS, **NOTHING STIRRED** HERE, NEAR THE BLACK COAST SOUTH OF **KUSH.**

THEN, WITH A GARGANTUAN EFFORT, THE MAN **RAISED** HIMSELF SLIGHTLY, PAINFULLY-- AS IF TO TEST IF HE STILL **LIVED.**

UNNNHH--!

NEXT, ROLLING CONVULSIVELY **OFF** THE DEAD BEAST, HE WAS NEARLY AS **UNMOVING** AS IT WAS... FOR A **LONG TIME.**

NOW-- THERE IS ONLY THE SLOW, MEASURED **BREATHING** OF THE SINEWY GIANT.

AT LEAST, THERE IS NO OTHER MOVEMENT **WITHIN** THIS MARSHY CIRCLE BENEATH THE DARK-GREEN CANOPY.

OTHER FORMS HOWEVER, MOVE TOWARD MAN AND APE...IN AN **EVER-CLOSING RING**...

...ONLY TO **HALT** SUDDENLY, AS IT TURNED TO MOTTLED **STONE**...

...AT THE ECHOING OF A SOUND **UNFAMILIAR** TO THE TRACKLESS, VINE-BESTREWN JUNGLE--

THE ROAR OF A **LION,** FAR FROM HIS VELDT HOME, PERHAPS--

GRARRR

--BUT STILL THE **MIGHTIEST** FELINE OF ALL!

SLOWLY, YET WITH A LORDLY DISDAIN FOR CAUTION, THE HUGE CAT PADS RELENTLESSLY *TOWARD* THE UNMOVING BARBARIAN, WHO *DOES NOT STIR*...

...TILL *HOT, FETID BREATH* LASHES OVER HIS BACK IN WAVES, AND A *LOW, HALF-SNARLING* PANTING IS IN HIS VERY EAR.

THEN, EVEN AS HE *WAKES*--

--HE *LEAPS AWAY*, DESPERATE FOR *LIFE!*

NAAAAHH!! GET OUT OF HERE!!

RRRR

YET, ALMOST INSTANTLY, EVEN IN HIS NEAR-PANIC, CONAN RECOGNIZES THE GREAT *BLACK LION* WHO WAS ONCE THE FAMILIAR COMPANION OF THE *ORIGINAL* JUNGLE-KING WHO BORE THE NAME OF *AMRA*...

AND, WHEN THE DARK BEAST *DOES NOT CHARGE*, BUT RATHER COMES MEEKLY FORWARD, WITH *HEAD* LOWERED FOR *PETTING*...

BONES OF CROM!

YOU HAIL ME AS AMRA, *TOO*, DON'T YOU-- FULL AS MUCH AS THE *SAVAGES* OF THE COAST!

GOT TO AC-KNOWLEDGE THAT... SOMEHOW...!

IT TAKES MORE COURAGE THAN EVEN *CONAN* USUALLY WISHES TO DISPLAY, TO DO WHAT HE DOES *NEXT*...

NICE LION! I BELIEVE *BÊLIT* SAID HE CALLED YOU-- *SHOLO!* *

SEE ISSUES #60-63. --ROY.

THEN, SATISFIED IN ITS OWN MYSTIC WAY, THE FELINE TURNS ITS ATTENTION TO THE FALLEN *BABOON*...

GOOD SHOLO! ENJOY YOUR *MEAL*, WITH MY *BEST* WISHES.

I'M SURE THAT WHEN YOU'RE *WELL FED* YOU'LL BE EVEN *LESS* A THREAT TO YOUR *MASTER*-BY-RIGHT-OF-*CONQUEST*...

61

STILL, I'LL FEEL BETTER WHEN I'VE A FEW FEET OF *COLD STEEL* TO PUT BETWEEN US... *JUST IN CASE.*

ALL THE SAME, NO NEED TO MAKE YOU FEEL *MENACED,* IS THERE?

NOW, AS HE *SHEATHES* HIS SWORD, THE CIMMERIAN THINKS BACK A MOMENT TO THE *STRANGE MISSION* WHICH HAS BROUGHT HIM HERE, TO THE ROCKY BACK-SIDE OF THE TIME-LOST CITY CALLED *ABOMBI*--

HE *SNARLS* TO HIMSELF AS HE RECALLS *AJAGA,* WHO HAS SOMEHOW GAINED THE EERIE POWER TO *CONTROL* MANY OF THE JUNGLE'S MOST FEROCIOUS *PREDATORS.*

AJAGA POSES THE *GREAT-EST THREAT,* BY FAR, TO HIS AND BÊLIT'S RE-ESTAB-LISHING THEMSELVES AS *MASTERS* OF THE BLACK COAST.

YET, WHEN THEY JOURNEYED UP THE NEARBY CLIFFS, THEY FOUND SEVERAL OF THE WARRIOR-KING'S *BEAST-MINIONS* WAITING FOR THEM--

AND NOW, THE HANDFUL OF *BLACK CORSAIRS* WHO CAME WITH THEM ARE DOUBTLESS *PRISONERS*-- OR *WORSE.*

BUT-- WHAT OF BÊLIT HERSELF?

IS SHE *DEAD,* CONAN WONDERS, AT THE HAND OF *AJAGA*--OR AT THE TALONS OF A *BABOON?*

IF SHE *IS,* HE VOWS SILENT-LY TO *THROTTLE* THE SO-CALLED *BEAST-KING* WITH HIS BARE, BRONZED *HANDS.*

STILL, BÊLIT I. *LOVELY,* IN HER WAY... AND IT'S SAID AJAGA HAS *MANY BRIDES* TO SERVE HIS NEEDS.

62

WELL, BEST TO WORRY ABOUT *THAT* WHEN HE'S CLOSER TO WITHIN *STRIKING-DISTANCE* OF THE MASTER OF ABOMBI...

UH, OUT OF MY WAY, SHOLO! I MUST BE--

DAMN! HE WON'T BUDGE.

THIS *JUNGLE LORD* THING ISN'T AS *SIMPLE* AS MY FORERUNNER MADE IT *LOOK*, IT SEEMS.

WHAT'S MORE, WHEN *I* MOVE, YOU COME ALONG *WITH* ME, DO YOU?

HO! MAYBE *YOU'RE* ANSWERING SOME *MYSTIC SUMMONS* FROM AJAGA, JUST LIKE YOUR *FELLOW BEASTS*, EH?

OF *COURSE!* WHY ELSE WOULD YOU BE SO FAR FROM YOUR *NATIVE HAUNTS*, WITH FIRST AMRA *SO LONG DEAD?*

THEN, *I'LL* JUST BE THE ONE TO TAG ALONG WITH *YOU*, GOOD SHOLO.

YOU'RE JUST LIABLE TO *LEAD* ME TO ABOMBI, BY SOME PATH WHERE I *WON'T* RUN AFOUL OF A SMALL ARMY OF *APES*.

NOT THAT ANYTHING MUCH SMALLER THAN AN *ELEPHANT* IS LIKELY TO BOTHER ME, WITH *YOU* AT MY SIDE.

RRRR

MEANWHILE, HIGH ABOVE THE *SOUND-ING SEA*...

...THE DAZED *PIRATE QUEEN* AWAKENS ON COLD AND UNYIELDING *FLAGSTONES*...

UHHH-- WHERE--?

...TO A SCENE OF *MAN* AMID *BEASTS* SUCH AS THE WORLD HAS NOT WITNESSED IN *MANY A CENTURY.*

AH, SO GOOD OF YOU TO *JOIN* US, "YOUR *MAJESTY.*"

YOU!

WHERE IS *AMRA*? WHERE ARE MY *CORSAIRS*?

MAY MY MOTHER, THE *DEATH-GODDESS DERKETA*, CALL DOWN *HELLFIRE* ON YOU, IF YOU DO NOT *BRING* THEM TO ME AT ONCE!

SEEK NOT TO FRIGHTEN *ME*, WOMAN, WITH BABBLINGS OF DESCENT FROM *DEATH-DEITIES* IN WHOM I DO NOT EVEN *BELIEVE!*

THERE IS *NO* POWER SOUTH OF KUSH BUT *AJAGA*-- HEIR TO THE LIVING THRONE OF *JHEBBAL SAG*, MASTER OF MEN AND BEASTS!*

*AS REFERRED TO IN *SAVAGE SWORD OF CONAN #27.* -- RT.

HER DARK EYES SHIFTING EVER SO SLIGHTLY, BÊLIT CAN SEE THAT THEIR LEADER'S DOUBLE BLASPHEMY MAKES EVEN THE TWO *WARRIOR-BROTHERS* AT HER BACK EXCEEDINGLY *UNEASY*... THOUGH THEY SAY NOTHING.

SHE FILES THE KNOWLEDGE AWAY... FOR A *LATER* TIME.

DO NOT SEEK TO HAVE ME *JOIN FORCES* WITH YOU, AJAGA.

I RULE THE BLACK COAST IN MY *OWN* WAY-- AND WITH A *LIGHTER HAND* THAN YOURS.

DOUBTLESS *SO*... FOR, I FOUND THAT *MOST* OF THE TRIBES I SUBDUED OR DESTROYED WOULD HAVE PREFERRED *YOUR* YOKE TO *MINE*.

STILL, I'VE *NO INTEREST* IN HAVING YOU JOIN ME...

...NOT EVEN AS ONE OF MY *RELUCTANT HOSTAGE-BRIDES*.

NO, I INTEND TO *SLAY* YOU...!

THEN DO SO *NOW*, JACKAL!

LET IT BE *YOU*-- OR *BÊLIT!*

NEITHER *KRATO* NOR *BEEYA* CAN LEAP FAST ENOUGH TO INTERCEPT THE SPRINGING PIRATE--

BUT, EVEN *HER* LITHE MOVEMENTS ARE AS A *SNAIL'S CRAWL* TO THE *SPOTTED PROTECTOR* WHICH HAS SAT PURRING, TILL THIS MOMENT AT AJAGA'S FEET...

RRRR

UNNNHH--!

NAY, MY *MOTTLED ONE!* DO *NOT* SLAY HER!

BETTER TO LET HER *BROOD* A WHILE, ON HER *HELP-LESSNESS*.

GUARDS! TAKE HER TO MY *DUNGEONS*-- FOR *NOW!*

WHY, O GREAT ONE, DO YOU NOT SIMPLY *SLIT HER THROAT*-- OR TURN HER OVER TO MY *BROTHER* AND ME?

BECAUSE, KRATO, I DO NOT *WISH* TO!

OH, SHE SHALL *DIE* SOON ENOUGH-- AND *PAINFULLY*--

--BUT *FIRST,* SHE MUST BE *EXHIBITED* LIKE A *PRIZE ANIMAL*-- IN AN IRON *CAGE*-- SO THAT ALL THE BLACK COAST MAY KNOW WHO IS ITS *TRUE* SOVEREIGN!

A *CURSE* ON YOU, DOG!

YOUR *OWN BEASTS* SHALL RISE UP AND *REND* YOU -- AND *BÊLIT* SHALL BE THERE!

DOES SHE *MEAN* AND *BELIEVE* THE WORDS-- OR ARE THEY SHEER *BRAVADO?*

AJAGA SEEMS NEITHER TO KNOW NOR TO CARE.

MEANWHILE, O AJAGA, THERE IS STILL THE MATTER OF THAT OLD *WITCH-FINDER*... THE ONE CALLED *G'CHAMBI.*

HE YET *DEFIES* US-- AND THERE ARE STILL THOSE IN THE JUNGLE WHO GIVE HIM *EAR.*

FEAR *NOT,* BEEYA.

HE HAS ALREADY BEEN... *ATTENDED* TO, HAS HE NOT, ISTO?

IN THERE, SHE-DEMON!

AS FOR *BÊLIT*-- SHE KNOWS THAT, MERELY BECAUSE OF AJAGA'S *WHIM,* SHE IS STILL *ALIVE*...

AND PERHAPS *THAT,* IN TIME, WILL PROVE *SUFFICIENT.*

IF *NOT*-- WELL--

--THEN BETTER TO BE A *DEAD QUEEN* OF MEMORY, THAN A *LIVING WRETCH,* SUCH AS THESE POOR SOULS WHO WERE ONCE THE *DAUGHTERS OF CHIEFTAINS!*

AND, ALL THIS WHILE, **CONAN THE BARBARIAN** WALKS WITH INCREASING EASE AND CONFIDENCE AT THE SIDE OF THE GREAT **BLACK LION.**

AS HE DOES SO, HE RECALLS THE WORDS OF THE **WATAMBI JUJU-MAN--**

ONCE, **ALL BEASTS** WORSHIPED THE STRANGE ENTITY KNOWN AS **JHEBBAL SAG--** IN THAT FAR-OFF DAY WHEN **MEN** AND **BEASTS** SPOKE THE SAME TONGUE.

TODAY, MEN HAVE LARGELY **FORGOTTEN** HIM....MEN, AND **MOST** ANIMALS.

BUT, **SOME** BEASTS STILL REMEMBER... AND THOSE WHO STILL REMEMBER, IN SOME DIM AND MYSTERIOUS WAY, **OBEY** THE SUMMONS OF **AJAGA.**

SHOLO, THINKS THE CIMMERIAN, IS ONE OF THOSE CREATURES WHO STILL **REMEMBER.**

FOR, **IGNORING** NERVOUS HYENAS THAT YIP AND YAP ABOVE THEIR PURLOINED MEAL, THE BIG CAT STRIDES WITH SOMBRE **PURPOSEFULNESS** THROUGH THE FOREST OF NIGHT.

SOMEHOW, CONAN **KNOWS** THAT SHOLO HEARS THE SIREN CALL OF THE **HEIR OF JHEBBAL SAG.**

AND HE **SMILES** GRIMLY TO HIMSELF TO WONDER IF PERHAPS HE SENSES THIS BECAUSE **HE TOO--** PRIMITIVE THAT HE IS-- IS **CLOSER** TO BEASTS THAN CIVILIZED MEN.

NO WAY OF KNOWING.

PERHAPS, AT ANY MOMENT, THE **LION** AT HIS SIDE WILL TURN **AGAINST** HIM UNDER AJAGA'S SPELL-- BUT CONAN WILL WORRY ABOUT THAT WHEN THE MOMENT **COMES.**

RIGHT NOW, HE SEES A **CAVE--** AND THOUGH HE IS SOME DISTANCE FROM THE BACK CLIFFS OF **ABOMBI,** HE THINKS PERHAPS IT **LEADS** SOMEWHERE.

PERHAPS EVEN TO **BÊLIT...** IF STILL SHE **LIVES!**

JUST THEN, ALL OF CONAN'S *FEARS* CONCERNING HIS FIERCE COMPANION SUDDENLY *WELL UP* INSIDE HIM, AS--

RRRARGG

WHAT *IS* IT, SHOLO?

HALTING IN ITS VERY *TRACKS*, THE GREAT CAT REFUSES TO GO *FURTHER*-- EVEN WHEN THE CIMMERIAN HIMSELF MOVES FORWARD--

--TO BEHOLD A *STRANGE SIGN* CARVED IN THE *SAND* BY THE RIVER'S EDGE.

HE HAS SEEN THAT WEIRD, INTRICATE SHAPE *BEFORE,* HE KNOWS...

...BUT *WHERE?*

MOVING CLOSER, STEP BY STEP, TO THE *CAVE,* HE YET LEAVES A CORNER OF HIS MIND BEHIND, TO DWELL ON THE UNMOVING *SHOLO.*

WHAT KIND OF *MAN-CARVED* SYMBOL IS IT THAT CAN FRIGHTEN A *BEAST* THAT CANNOT READ?

AS HE *ENTERS* THE YAWNING DARKNESS, CONAN IS ALMOST *GLAD* THE LION HAS STAYED BEHIND... FOR *MORE* REASONS THAN ONE.

FOR, WITH ITS GREATER *BULK,* THE HUGE CARNIVORE COULD HARDLY HAVE SCRAMBLED *SILENTLY* OVER THE LOOSE ROCK AND SHALE WITHIN...

...WHILE *HE,* TEAMING A PANTHER'S FLUID GRACE WITH A WOLF'S TENSE FURY, GLIDES INTO BLACKNESS LIKE ONE MORE *SHADOW AMONG SHADOWS.*

YET, FOR ALL *THAT*--

WELCOME, O *AMRA*!

WHAT--?

IF THAT'S *YOU* OR YOUR *DEVILS*, *AJAGA*, COME FORTH AND I'LL--

NAY, NAY, LORD OF LIONS...OLD *G'CHAMBI* IS NOT ONE OF *AJAGA'S* MINIONS.

OH, HE'D *LIKE* ME TO BE! HOW HE'D *LOVE* G'CHAMBI TO TELL THE *YOUNG MEN* TO FOLLOW HIM, AND THE *OLD* TO GIVE UP THEIR *FREEDOM* AND THEIR *DAUGHTERS*! BUT I--

G'CHAMBI?! I'VE-- *HEARD* THAT NAME--!

BUT, WHO *ARE* YOU, THAT SOUND LIKE AS MUCH A *FOE* OF AJAGA'S AS *I*?

WAS IT *YOU* WHO SCRATCHED THAT *SYMBOL* IN THE SAND OUTSIDE?

AH, SO YOU *NOTICED* IT, DID YOU?

AS DID YOUR *BLACK LION*-- AS IT *EVER* DID, WHEN YOU AND IT DREW NEAR MY CAVE IN THE *OLD DAYS*!

HMMM... I THINK I AM *NOT* THE "*AMRA*" YOU REMEMBER, OLD MAN-- BUT I RECALL HEARING OF *YOU*-- A *WITCH-FINDER* OF SOME REPUTE IN TIMES PAST!

AYE! THAT'S WHY AJAGA WANTS ME EITHER TO *HEEL*-- OR ELSE TO *DIE*.

HE KNOWS HIS BEASTS WILL NOT COME *NEAR* ME, WHILE THE SIGN OF *JHEBBAL SAG* IS SCRATCHED OUTSIDE-- AND HIS *MEN* FEAR MY *JUJU*!

WAIT! I JUST RECALLED-- WHERE I *SAW* THAT SIGN BEFORE--!

"IT WAS IN THE *UNINHABITED* MOUNTAINS, BEYOND THE *VILAYET SEA*-- HALF A WORLD FROM HERE!

"*YES*! IT WAS CARVED IN THE *ROCK* OF A CAVE NO MAN HAD VISITED FOR A *MILLION YEARS*; I KNEW THAT, SOMEHOW, EVEN AS I *STOOD* BEFORE IT!

CAN *I* USE THAT SYMBOL, THEN, TO LIKEWISE HOLD AJAGA'S CREATURES *AT BAY*-- SO I CAN RESCUE MY *WOMAN*?

WELL? *ANSWER* ME, OLD MAN?

ARE WE ON THE *SAME SIDE*, YOU AND I, OR--?

SUDDENLY, A **SCREAM OUT OF HELL** ECHOES THROUGH THE ETERNAL NIGHT OF THE CAVE--

AAAAAA

G'CHAMBI--?

WHERE HAVE YOU **GONE,** CURSE YOU?!

BAD ENOUGH HAVING TO **TALK** TO YOU IN **PITCH-DARKNESS,** WITHOUT--

BY MITRA, IF THIS IS SOME **WITCH-MAN'S TRICK,** I'LL SEPARATE YOUR ANCIENT **HEAD** FROM YOUR SCRAWNY **SHOULDERS!**

BUT, AN INSTANT **LATER--**

UNNGN

--THE OLD MAN'S **CLAWED AND BLEEDING FORM,** LIMP AND UN-MOVING, IS TOSSED INTO SUCH **DIM LIGHT** AS THERE IS!

AND, TURNING HIS STRAINING EYES **UPWARD** TO WHERE THE OLD MAN STOOD A FEW MOMENTS BEFORE-- HE ABRUPTLY BEHOLDS THE **NIGHT-MARISH THING** WHICH HAS TORN G'CHAMBI VIRTUALLY TO **SHREDS...!**

CROM'S DEVILS!

GRONK

WHATEVER THE CREATURE IS, CONAN CAN TELL EVEN IN THE TWILIGHT THAT IT IS POISED TO **LEAP** AGAIN AT THE **WITCH-FINDER...**

...EVEN AS AN ALMOST INAUDIBLE **GROAN** TELLS THE BARBARIAN THAT G'CHAMBI IS **STILL ALIVE!**

HERE, OLD PIG-SWALLOWER!

CHEW ON **THIS** A WHILE!

HRRK?

HRONKK

HOLY ISHTAR!

GRAAK

THE MAN-SIZED SAURIAN'S BODY, EVEN ITS **BELLY,** IS HEAVILY **ARMORED** -- AND, THOUGH CONAN'S SHARP BLADE SLICES **THROUGH** ITS SCALES --

--THERE IT **STICKS,** SOLIDLY ENOUGH TO BE PULLED FROM EVEN THE BRAWNY **CIMMERIAN'S** IRON GRIP!

=MMFF--!=

AND, WHEN IT COMES **OUT** AGAIN AMID THE LIZARD-THING'S FLAILINGS

--IT MIGHT AS WELL BE A *UNIVERSE AWAY* FROM ITS FORMER WIELDER!

GRRG

YOU'RE *STRONG*, DEVIL-- STRONGER THAN *ME!*

BUT YOU'RE STILL A *BEAST*-- NOT A *MAN*--

FRONNK

--AND YOU'VE NOT BEEN *WRESTLING* SINCE YOU WERE KNEE- HIGH TO A *SNOW-BEAR!*

IN AN INSTANT, A *DESPERATE HAND* REACHES FOR THE *COLD STEEL BLADE* WHICH LIES, UNCARING, ON THE STONES...

...BUT *REACHES*, ALAS, A *SPLIT- SECOND TOO SLOWLY!*

HRONK

¿AGGHH--!¡

THAT GREAT *BEAK*-- MORE LIKE A GIANT *BIRD'S* THAN A LIZARD'S-- WOULD NOW BITE *INTO* AND CLEANLY *THROUGH* ITS PREY'S SHOULDER--

--SAVE THAT, *SENSING* THIS, CONAN MANAGES INSTEAD TO PULL ITS HEAD AND NECK TOO FAR *FORWARD*--

AND, A MOMENT LATER, THE SAURIAN'S OWN VASTER *SIZE* AND *WEIGHT*--

--BECOMES AT ONCE ITS GREATEST *LIABILITY,* AS ALL THAT BULK MERELY ADDS TO *CONAN'S* OWN IN SMASHING ITS *HEAD* AGAINST UNYIELDING *STONE!*

GR-KK

STILL, THE CIMMERIAN KNOWS HE CANNOT *WIN* THIS UNEVEN BATTLE, IN THE END--

--NOT WHILE IT WAVERS IN THE *BALANCE,* TO BE DECIDED BY SHEER *STRENGTH* AGAINST *STRENGTH!*

HE MUST *WEAKEN* THE MONSTER-- BY STRIKING IT *YET AGAIN* UPON THE HARD STONE, WHILE PRAYING WORDLESSLY THAT IT HAS ENOUGH OF A *BRAIN* TO BE *DAMAGED!*

RONK

BUT STILL, THE LIZARD-THING *WRITHES* MADLY, WITH SUCH *RAW, UNTAMED POWER* AS MEN WOULD TRADE THEIR UNTRAMMELLED *SOULS* TO POSSESS.

CONAN'S *MAN-KNOWLEDGE* ENABLES HIM, FOR A SECOND ONLY, TO HURL THE CREATURE TO THE *CAVERN FLOOR*--

--KNOWING, EVEN AS HE DOES SO, THAT HE MUST SURELY *DIE* IF EVER IT *RISES* AGAIN!

ON HIS **DAY OF MANHOOD**, A DECADE AGONE, YOUNG CONAN BROKE THE NECK OF A **WILD BULL.**

HRONK

THAT FEAT WAS TO **THIS**--AS THE LANDING OF A **MINNOW** IS TO THE SLAYING OF A **SNARK.**

YET, AT LENGTH, THE CORSAIR HEARS THE TELLTALE **CRACK** BENEATH HIS SUN-BRONZED SINEWS-- A SOUND WHICH CAN HAVE BUT **ONE MEANING**--

--AND THE GREAT SAURIAN'S FRAME GOES **LIMP**, AS THOUGH IT WERE A **DOLL** WHOSE NECK HE HAD JUST BROKEN!

ITS **TAIL** THRASHES ONCE...THEN AGAIN, MORE SLOWLY...

...AND THEN IS **STILL.**

AND, EVEN AS HE **RISES**, RACKED WITH PAIN, TO HIS FEET, CONAN IS SUDDENLY ALL BUT **OVERWHELMED** BY THE AWESOME AND HORRIFYING **KNOWLEDGE**--

--KNOWLEDGE THAT THE LIZARD-THING WAS **SENT** HERE THROUGH SOME LONG-NEGLECTED **ENTRANCE** FORGOTTEN EVEN BY OLD **G'CHAMBI**--

--SENT HERE BY SOME SECRET PATH THAT **AVOIDED** THE MYSTIC SYMBOL OF **JHEBBAL SAG**--

--SENT BY **AJAGA!!**

NEVER HAS EVEN THE *JUNGLE NIGHT* LOOKED SO *INVITING* AS IT DOES TO CONAN UPON EMERGING FROM THAT HAUNTED *DEATH-CAVE*...

...TO CARRY A DYING *G'CHAMBI* TO A SPOT WELL OUT IN THE *OPEN.*

SO, SHOLO-- NOW YOU DRAW NEAR, SINCE WE'RE *FURTHER* FROM THE SAND SYMBOL, EH?

BLAME *NOT*... YOUR LION... AMRA!

HE KNOWS... THE *POWER*... OF JHEBBAL SAG.

YOU MEAN-- THE *SIGN*?!

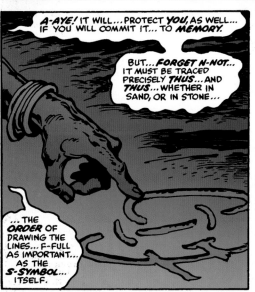

A-AYE! IT WILL...PROTECT *YOU*, AS WELL... IF YOU WILL COMMIT IT...TO *MEMORY.*

BUT... *FORGET N-NOT...* IT MUST BE TRACED PRECISELY *THUS*...AND *THUS*...WHETHER IN SAND, OR IN STONE...

...THE *ORDER* OF DRAWING THE LINES... F-FULL AS IMPORTANT... AS THE *S-SYMBOL...* ITSELF.

REMEMBER IT, AMRA...THAT IT MAY *SHIELD* YOU... F-FROM THE *DEVILS*...WHO *SERVE* THE D-DEVIL...AJAGGGGGK※…

CONAN WISHES THE OLD MAN HAD LIVED LONG ENOUGH TO TELL *WHY* HE PRE- FERRED TO *DEFY* AJAGA, RATHER THAN SERVE HIM AND REAP A RICH *REWARD.*

PERHAPS IT WAS SOME *NOBLE* REASON...

OR PERHAPS, CONAN THINKS, THE OLD MAN WAS JUST PLAIN *STUBBORN.*

AT ANY RATE, NO FOUR-FOOTED *SCAVENGERS* SHALL DISTURB THE BONES OF POOR, DEAD *G'CHAMBI.*

AND AS FOR *AJAGA*--

WELL, CONAN OF CIMMERIA IS LOOKING FORWARD TO *MEETING* THAT WORTHY *AGAIN*...

...LOOKING FORWARD TO IT VERY, VERY *MUCH!*

NEXT ISSUE: **THE LONG NIGHT** OF FANG AND TALON!

"Know, O prince, that between the years when the oceans drank Atlantis and the gleaming cities, and the rise of the sons of Aryas, there was an Age undreamed of, when shining kingdoms lay spread across the world like blue mantles beneath the stars.
"Hither came Conan, the Cimmerian, black-haired, sullen-eyed, sword in hand, a thief, a reaver, a slayer, with gigantic melancholies and gigantic mirth, to tread the jeweled thrones of the Earth under his sandaled feet."
—The Nemedian Chronicles.

Stan Lee PRESENTS: CONAN THE BARBARIAN™

THE LONG NIGHT OF FANG AND TALON! PART ONE

ONCE, SOME THREE YEARS AGO, A RED-TRESSED *AQUILONIAN* LORD WALKED THESE JUNGLES *SOUTH OF KUSH* -- A GREAT, BLACK-MANED *LION* SNARLING SAVAGELY AT HIS SIDE -- AND WAS CALLED *AMRA*.

TONIGHT, A DARK-HAIRED *BARBARIAN* OUT OF *CIMMERIA* STALKS THE SHADOW-HAUNTED FOREST, THAT SAME *BLACK LION* PADDING REGALLY BEFORE HIM.

AND *THIS* MAN, TOO, IS *AMRA*... WHOSE NAME *MEANS* "LION"...!

ROY THOMAS * JOHN BUSCEMA & ERNIE CHAN
WRITER/EDITOR — ILLUSTRATORS

JOE ROSEN, LETTERER — JIM SHOOTER CONSULTING EDITOR

FEATURING THE HERO CREATED BY ROBERT E. HOWARD

CONAN IS **NEARLY** AT EASE NOW IN THE PRESENCE OF THE HUGE **CARNIVORE**...

YET, HE STILL KEEPS HIS **SWORD-HAND** READY TO GRASP HIS BLADE'S FIRM **HILT**...

...AS HIS MIND WANDERS TO THE **CAPTURE OF BÊLIT**, ALONG WITH SEVERAL OF HER CORSAIRS, BY THE BLACK WARRIOR-KING NAMED **AJAGA**...

...HE WHO CAN SPEAK TO AND COMMAND MANY FIERCE **JUNGLE BEASTS**, AND CALLS HIMSELF THE **HEIR OF JHEBBAL SAG.**

AGAIN HE RE-LIVES THEIR BRIEF EN-COUNTER WITH THE SELF-STYLED **BEAST KING** --

THE SICKENING **FALL**, ALONG WITH TWO SNARLING **BABOONS**, SERVANTS OF AJAGA, FROM A **CLIFF** BEHIND THE LOST CITY OF **ABOMBI**...

...WITH ONLY THE **TREES**, THE SWAMPY **MARSH**, AND AN APE'S YIELDING **CORPSE** TO SAVE HIM FROM A BONE-SHATTERING **DEATH.**

THAT WAS WHEN **SHOLO** CAME ONTO THE SCENE... **SHOLO**, WHO ONCE SERVED THE **FIRST** AMRA, LONG AGO...

...AND NOW HONORS **CONAN** AS THE **SECOND AMRA.** *

* SEE #60-63. --ROY.

STILL, IT IS **NOT** THE WISHES OF **CONAN** THAT THE GREAT BLACK LION FOLLOWS **THIS** NIGHT...

YOU STILL HEAR AND HEED THE **SUMMONS OF AJAGA**, DON'T YOU, SHOLO?

WELL, **I'VE** YET HOPE THAT YOU WILL **LEAD** ME TO AJAGA, AND TO BÊLIT, BY SOME **SECRET WAY** THROUGH THE CLIFFS.

I JUST **WONDER** WHAT WILL HAPPEN-- IF AND WHEN THE BEAST-KING ORDERS YOU TO TURN ON **ME!**

JUST THEN, AS IF ON SOME *MYSTICAL CUE* THAT ONLY THE *DARK FELINE* ITSELF HAS SENSED--

RRARR

CROM'S DEVILS!

BUT, THE *ATTACK* THE CIMMERIAN FEARS DOES *NOT* COME.

IT SEEMS TO BE ONLY THE *LION'S INSTINCTS*, VENTING THEMSELVES IN THE *JUNGLE NIGHT.*

YET, NEXT MOMENT, CONAN SEES--

A *CAVE!* IS *THAT* WHY YOU ROARED, CAT?

IS THIS OUR WAY THROUGH TO *ABOMBI* ON THE OTHER SIDE, OR--?

DAMN! I WISH *I* COULD UNDERSTAND YOU, THE WAY *AJAGA* PROBABLY COULD.

ALL THE SAME, IF *YOU* GO IN-- IT *MUST* BE BECAUSE YOU FOLLOW THE BEAST-KING'S *SILENT CALL.*

HE'D BE *PLEASED,* NO DOUBT, TO ADD A *LION* TO HIS MOTLEY HORDE OF *BABOONS, SNAKES, HAWKS,* AND *LEOPARDS.*

GUESS I'LL NEVER KNOW *WHY* SOME ANIMALS STILL *UNDERSTAND* THE STRANGE ANCIENT *TONGUE* AJAGA SPEAKS IN HIS MADNESS-- WHILE MOST OTHERS HAVE *FORGOTTEN* IT.

MY EYES AREN'T *QUITE* AS SHARP AS YOURS IN THE DARK, SHOLO-- SO I'LL JUST LIGHT A *TORCH* WITH TINDER MATERIALS I BROUGHT ALONG FROM THE *WATAMBI VILLAGE.*

I KNOW *YOU* DON'T LIKE FIRE MUCH-- BUT I COULD USE THE *HELP*--

RRRR

--TO KEEP FROM TOPPLING OFF THE *SUDDEN CLIFFS* THAT ABOUND IN THIS ACCURSED PLACE!

MITRA! IF ONLY I DARED TAKE THE TIME TO RETURN TO THE *SHIP,* AND SAIL WITH OUR *BLACK PIRATES* AGAINST ABOMBI!

BUT, THAT WOULD ONLY **ALERT** AJAGA-- AND BÊLIT AND THE OTHERS WOULD BE **DEAD** BEFORE THE FIRST CORSAIR HAD SET FOOT IN HIS **RE-CLAIMED CITY.**

SO, I GUESS IT'S UP TO **YOU AND ME**, LION, TO--

WHAT THE DEVIL--?

AND, IT SEEMS THAT IT HAS **SUFFICED--**

BOTH **BEAST** AND **BARBARIAN** CAN BE FORGIVEN FOR NOT SENSING THAT THE SEEMINGLY **SOLID ROCK** BENEATH THEIR FEET WOULD SUDDENLY **GIVE WAY** BENEATH THEM...

FOR, IT IS A **TRAP** OF AJAGA'S-- MEANT TO KEEP **ANY FOEMEN** FROM CREEPING UPON THE RUINS OF ABOMBI **UNDETECTED.**

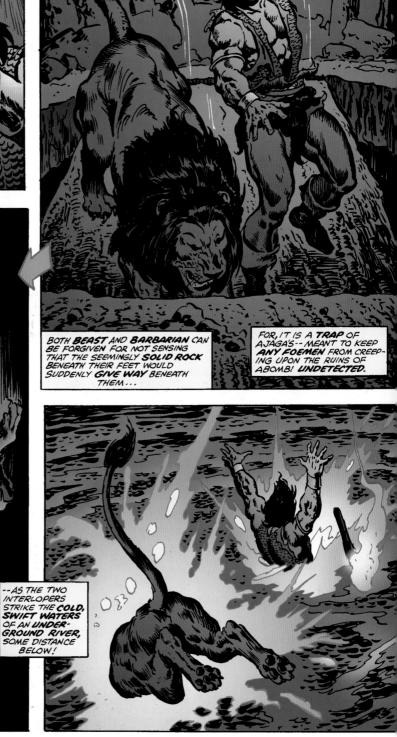

--AS THE TWO INTERLOPERS STRIKE THE **COLD, SWIFT WATERS** OF AN **UNDERGROUND RIVER,** SOME DISTANCE BELOW!

RRRR

78

--INTO *UTTER, ABYSMAL DARKNESS* ARE THEY PLUNGED, WITHOUT WARNING!

FOR A PASSING MOMENT, CONAN IS CONCERNED FOR *SHOLO*-- FOR, DESPITE HIS GREAT STRENGTH, THE HUGE CARNIVORE IS DOUBTLESS, LIKE HIS KIND, A *POOR SWIMMER.*

ONLY THE *TIGERS OF VENDHYA,* IT IS SAID, TAKE TO WATER LIKE *STRIPED SHARKS.*

NEXT MOMENT, HOWEVER, ALL THOUGHTS OF THE BLACK LION *FLY* FROM HIS MIND--

--AS A FAINT *SPECK OF LIGHT,* MOVING IN HIS DIRECTION, SUDDENLY BECOMES A *WRITHING, PHOSPHORESCENT MENACE!*

--BUT NEVER UP SO *CLOSE*--

-- NOR *STREAKING* MALEVOLENTLY, *RAGGED JAWS* OPEN WIDE, FOR HIS *OWN FACE!*

CONAN HAS SEEN SUCH GLOWING *"SEA SERPENTS,"* WHICH HE KNOWS ARE *NOT* SNAKES AT ALL, BUT *GIGANTIC EELS,* FROM THE DECKS OF THE OCEAN-ROVING *TIGRESS*--

HIS METAL BLADE *SLICES DOWN* THROUGH THE RUSHING RIVER--

--AND IT IS AS IF HE HAS *STRUCK A THUNDERBOLT,* OR TRIED TO SPEAR *HEAVEN'S OWN LIGHTNING!*

ONLY THE *NIGHT-FREEZING* WATERS STIFLE HIS OWN CRY OF *ANGUISH.*

THEN, HURTLING **AWAY** FROM THE UNDULATING CREATURE, HE COLLIDES WITH A **SUNKEN BOULDER.**

AND, WITH A DESPERATE **STRENGTH**-- CONCEIVED IN **FEAR** AND MIDWIFED BY **COURAGE**-- HE STANDS HIS GROUND BEFORE THE CHARGING SEA-BEAST--

--TO USE THE JAGGED-EDGED, MASSIVE ROCK AS A **WEAPON!**

UP AGAINST THE UNDERWATER **CLIFF-WALL** HE SHOVES THE BOULDER-- CATCHING THE VIOLENTLY STRUGGLING EEL 'TWIXT **STONE** AND **STONE!**

A FEW **SECONDS** OF THIS, AND EVEN THE **MONSTER** MUST DIE-- **CRUSHED** BY THE RELENTLESS **WEIGHT** PRESSED AGAINST IT--

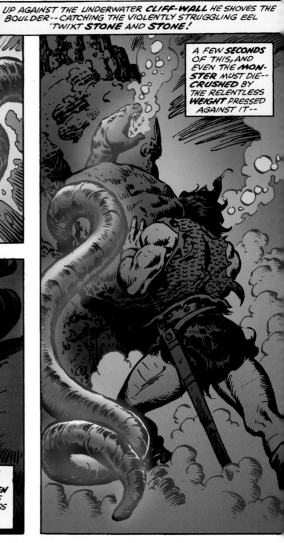

--**IF** ITS HUMAN ATTACKER DOES NOT PERISH **FIRST**--

--FROM LACK OF THE LIFE-GIVING **OXYGEN** FOR WHICH HIS BURSTING LUNGS **SCREAM IN SILENCE!**

ONE **FINAL** FRANTIC SHOVE BY CONAN--

--THE **PRESSURE** OF THE RAGGED BOULDER SLICING THE HUGE EEL **IN TWO** AT LAST--

--THEN THE STONE **DROPS** FROM BRONZED HANDS THAT NO LONGER **FEEL** ITS WEIGHT--

--AS A MIGHTY FORM FLOATS **UPWARD**, LIKE A CHILD'S RUBBER BALL, AWAY FROM THE **DYING GLOW** OF THE "SEA-SERPENT" WRIGGLING IN ITS DEATH-THROES BELOW--

-- AND TOWARD WHAT SHOULD BE THE **TOTAL BLACKNESS** OF THE **RIVER-SHORE** ABOVE.

YET, ALL IS **NOT** SHEER DARKNESS-- NOT **QUITE**--

--AS THE WAVERING LIGHT OF A **SINGLE TORCH** COMES NEARER, MOMENT BY MOMENT--

--TILL AT LENGTH A LARGE **EBON HAND** GRASPS THE BOBBING CIMMERIAN BY HIS **WET MANE.**

I **HAVE** HIM, CHIEF KRATO!

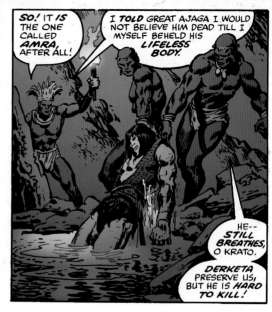

SO! IT **IS** THE ONE CALLED **AMRA**, AFTER ALL!

I **TOLD** GREAT AJAGA I WOULD NOT BELIEVE HIM DEAD TILL I MYSELF BEHELD HIS **LIFELESS BODY.**

HE-- **STILL BREATHES**, O KRATO.

DERKETA PRESERVE US, BUT HE IS **HARD TO KILL!**

PERHAPS! STILL, A *SINGLE KNIFE-THRUST* WOULD SOON DO THE TRICK--

--IF I DID NOT ANTICIPATE THE *WILL OF AJAGA!* COME....!

ERE LONG, IN ONE OF THE DANK *INNER CHAMBERS* OF THIS TIME-LOST CITY BY THE SEA...

YOU HAVE SERVED ME *WELL* TO BRING AMRA TO ME *ALIVE*, KRATO.

HE WILL FIT NICELY INTO MY *PLANS* TO BRING ALL THE *BLACK COAST* UNDER OUR SWAY!

MY BROTHER *ERRED*, O GREAT ONE! HE SHOULD HAVE BROUGHT YOU AMRA'S *HEAD*, MERELY-- AND LEFT HIS BODY FOR THE *FISH* TO GNAW!

NO, BEEYA!

I HAVE MY *OWN* WAY OF DOING THESE THINGS.

AND I AM *JOYED* THAT MY RIVAL *SURVIVED*...

...FOR, WHEN I FIRST *EXHIBIT*, THEN *SACRIFICE* BOTH AMRA AND BÊLIT TOGETHER-- ALL THE JUNGLE WILL BOW DOWN AT LAST BEFORE *AJAGA*, HEIR TO THE *MANTLE* OF *JHEBBAL SAG!*

BÊLIT...!?

WHERE IS BÊLIT??

BY THE GODS! HE RECOVERS-- SO QUICKLY--!

GIVE HER TO ME, JACKALS-- AND *ALIVE*--

--OR I'LL *BATHE* THIS ROOM IN YOUR *BLOOD*, SWORD OR NO!!

EVEN AS HE LEAPS TO HIS FEET, CONAN HEARS A SAVAGE *SNARL*--

--AND HE SEES WITH A *SHOCK* THAT IT EMANATES *NOT* FROM THE LITHE *LEOPARD* AT THE BEAST-KING'S SIDE --

RARRGH!

--BUT FROM THE *THROAT* OF *AJAGA* HIMSELF!

82

NEXT MOMENT, HIS **LEOPARD FAMILIAR** GIVES OUT AN ANSWERING SNARL-- EVEN AS IT **LEAPS** TO THE ATTACK!

FEW ARE THE MEN OR BEASTS WHICH COULD HOPE TO EVADE, EVEN FOR AN INSTANT, THE TALONS OF A HURTLING *PANTHER*...

BUT, *CONAN* OF *CIMMERIA* IS ONE OF THOSE FEW...

...AND THE *BLOW* WITH WHICH HE BUFFETS THE CAT, WHICH WOULD *CRUSH* MOST HUMAN SKULLS, SENDS THE ANIMAL WRITHING TO THE CHAMBER FLOOR!

*ANOTHER SECOND, AND THE LEOPARD WOULD BE **UP** AGAIN-- AND EVEN **CONAN** COULD DOUBT-LESS NOT EVADE IT A **SECOND** TIME...*

...ERE IS TO **BE** NO SECOND TIME, HOWEVER...

CORSAIR DOG!

UNNH

WELL DONE! I DO NOT WANT THE OUTLANDER'S FLESH TORN BY MY MOTTLED PET... NOT JUST *YET.*

AND NOW, IT IS TIME I CONSULTED *JHEBBAL SAG* HIMSELF-- IN THE *NETHERWORLD* WHERE HE HAS DWELT THESE PAST MILLENNIA--

-- TO LEARN *HIS* WILL, WITH REGARDS TO *AMRA* AND *BÊLIT!*

A HEARTBEAT LATER, IT IS AS IF AN **UNSEEN THUNDERBOLT** STRIKES THE SELF-STYLED **MASTER** OF ABOMBI...

YYAAA

...AND HE **TOPPLES** TO THE FLOOR, WHEREON HE WRITHES AND TWISTS FOR LONG MINUTES, WHILE UTTERING INARTICULATE **SCREAMS**.

JHEBBAL SAG!

NORSTRO AJAGA--

THEN, AS SUDDENLY AS IT CAME, THE DIVINE MADNESS **LEAVES** HIM... AND HE IS **HIMSELF** ONCE AGAIN...

...AMONG **FOLLOWERS** AS AWED AS FOLLOWERS **ALWAYS** ARE, IN THE PRESENCE OF A **HOLY ONE**.

THEN--

JHEBBAL SAG HAS SPOKEN TO ME!

AMRA AND BÊLIT MUST B SACRIFICED-- AT ONCE!

MEANWHILE, WHAT OF THE LEONINE **SHOLO**-- SWEPT ON BY THE UNDERGROUND RIVER INTO WHICH HE AND CONAN BOTH FELL?

HE IS **FAR** ALREADY FROM THE SITE WHERE THE BRONZE-SKINNED AMRA BATTLED THE **GIANT EEL**, AND STRUGGLING HARD TO **KEEP AFLOAT**--

--WHEN A KINDLY **FATE** SWEEPS HIM UP ON A ROCKY SHORE, WHERE HE RISES, SNARLING AND BRUISED IN THE NEAR-TOTAL DARKNESS.

STILL, ALL THIS WHILE, HE HAS HEARD THE SILENT **CALL** OF AJAGA...

FOR A TIME, ONLY **BLIND INSTINCT** LEADS HIM ON-- FOR SUDDENLY, THE INNER CALL **CEASES,** INTERRUPTED BY THE **SWOONING TRANCE** INTO WHICH, SOME DISTANCE AWAY, AJAGA HAS FALLEN.

THUS, THE GREAT **BLACK LION** FOLLOWS... **OTHER** SENSES.

AS, ELSEWHERE, IN A LOCKED CELL...

WELL? WON'T ANY OF YOU EVEN **ANSWER** ME?

HAS AJAGA'S **LEOPARD** STOLEN ALL YOUR **TONGUES?**

YOU WERE ONCE THE **DAUGHTERS OF CHIEFTAINS,** ALL OF YOU-- YET NOW YOU MEEKLY ACCEPT THE FACT THAT YOU ARE **LOVE-SLAVES** OF THAT SELF-PROCLAIMED BEAST-KING!

I SAY TO YOU, HOWEVER, THAT HE IS MORE **BEAST** THAN **KING!**

WE CAN **BREAK OUT** OF THIS HELLHOLE, IF WE ALL ACT **TOGETHER!**

MORE **SILENCE.**

WHAT OF **YOU,** NYAMI? YOU'RE THE DAUGHTER OF THE **CHIEF OF THE WATAMBIS--!**

AND **YOU** ARE THE DAUGHTER OF THE **DEATH-GODDESS** HERSELF-- YET YOU TOO ARE **HELPLESS.**

WHAT HOPE IS THERE, THEN, FOR **ANY** OF US?

FOR THE FIRST TIME, BÊLIT REALIZES THAT THE **PLOY** OF HER OLD MENTOR N'YAGA, WHICH HAS MADE HER A VIRTUAL **DEITY** ON THE BLACK COAST-- HAS **BACKFIRED** ON HER...

AJAGA **TAKES** THOSE HE WANTS-- AND **SACRIFICES** THE REST TO HIS BEASTS, AFTER HIS **MEN** ARE DONE WITH US.

YOUR FATE WILL BE THE **SAME...!**

NO!

BY DERKETA, **NO** MAN WILL TOUCH ME UNLESS I **WANT** HIM TO--

--AND **NO BEAST** WILL GNAW MY BONES!

YET, EVEN SHE CAN HEAR THE HOLLOW **MOCKERY** IN HER WORDS, RESOUNDING LIKE A VAGRANT ECHO IN THIS CELL WHERE **SHE** IS AS MUCH A PRISONER AS ANY.

ONLY **ACTION** NOW WILL SOOTHE THE WILD **FIRES** WHICH RAGE WITHIN HER-- **ANY** ACTION-- AND SO--

YES! I'LL GET FREE OF THIS PLACE-- I **SWEAR** IT--

-- OR JOIN MY **DEATH-GODDESS MOTHER** IN THE TRYING!

BÊLIT IS **STRONG**-- BUT THE BARS, THOUGH ANCIENT, ARE UNYIELDING.

BUT THEN, EVEN AS **BLACKNESS** SWIMS OVER HER EYES-- SHE ABRUPTLY FEELS A HARSH, WET, RASPING **TOUCH** ON HER FINGERTIPS--

EEYAAAH--!

AND PERHAPS SHE **WOULD** BURST HER HEART, AND **DIE**, ERE LONG--

--AND REACTS MUCH AS **ANY** MORTAL WOULD, IN ANY TIME OR CLIME--

--ENDING UP IN A MANNER MOST UN-**FITTING** TO DAUGHTERS OF DOOM-SPIRITS!

OOOOF

STILL, WHEN THE CREATURE BEYOND THE BARS MOVES INTO THE DIM LIGHT, SHE RECOGNIZES **SHOLO**-- WHO ONCE BOWED HIS DARK MANE BEFORE **CONAN!**

PERHAPS IT IS MERE- LY A DESPERATE **PRIDE** WHICH NEEDS REFURBISHING-- IF SHE'S TO RE-ESTABLISH HER- SELF AS A **GODDESS** IN THE EYES OF HER FELLOW INMATES.

OR, PERHAPS IT IS THE LIGHT OF AN INSPIRED *REASON.*

WHATEVER IT BE, BÊLIT FORCES HERSELF TO REACH OUT AND LIGHTLY *TOUCH* THE HUGE CARNIVORE...

NICE... SHOLO...!

...AND FINDS HIM *FRIENDLY* TO ONE HE REMEMBERS AS THE *MATE OF AMRA.*

THANK ISHTAR! NOW, IF ONLY I CAN MAKE YOU *UNDER-STAND*--

--THAT I WANT TO-- *MUST* GET OUT OF HERE--!

≈UNNNHH--!≈

AND SHOLO *DOES* UNDERSTAND, IN HIS WAY-- RESPONDING WITH MIGHTY JAWS WHICH CAN CRUSH THE HEAD OF A *BABOON* AS IF IT WERE AN EGGSHELL--

--SO THAT, WITHIN SECONDS--!

RRR

WOMEN OF *KUSH!* YOU HAVE SEEN THAT EVEN *LIONS* OBEY ME-- AS MUCH AS ANY WILD BEASTS OBEY *AJAGA!*

WILL YOU *FOLLOW* ME, NOW-- AND STRIKE AS YOUR *WARRIOR-FATHERS* WOULD?

NO, DAUGHTER OF DERKETA! YOU GO BUT TO YOUR *DOOM*-- YOURS AND *AMRA'S!*

WE HAVE SEEN *MORE* OF AJAGA'S POWER THAN YOU-- AND WE'LL NOT *OPPOSE* IT!

AYE! IF WE STAY HERE-- WE *MAY* LIVE-- PROVIDING WE *PLEASE* AJAGA!

TO GO WITH *YOU*-- IS TO RUN TO *DEATH!*

O AJAGA! THE SHE-PIRATE IS **GONE**-- ESCAPED SOMEHOW FROM THE WOMEN'S CELL!

ONE OF THE **BARS** WAS PULLED OUT, AS IF BY--

ENOUGH! THE FEMALE DOES **NOT** CONCERN ME NOW!

LET HER IRON-THEWED **MATE** DIE, AND BÊLIT WILL BE **NO MORE** THE QUEEN OF THE BLACK COAST, FLED OR NOT!

THEN, LONG SPEAR IN HAND, AJAGA SCRATCHES THE MAGICAL **SYMBOL OF JHEBBAL SAG** IN THE STONE AND DUST BEFORE HIM--

--THAT ANCIENT, MYSTIC SIGN WHICH EVEN THE **WILDEST** ANIMAL IS COWED BEFORE, AND DRAWS NOT NEAR.

IT WILL KEEP HIS **HUMAN MINIONS** SAFE...

...WHEN HE HAS SUMMONED HIS **FANGED AND TALONED** SERVITORS, WITH HIS GREAT **TRUMPET** MADE FROM THE THIGH-BONE OF A **REPTILE** LONG EXTINCT--

...BUT WHICH, IN EONS PAST, BOWED DOWN TO **JHEBBAL SAG**, FIRST MASTER OF MEN AND BEASTS!

AND, AS THE SOUND **ECHOES** THROUGHOUT THE CAVERNS, CONAN **AWAKES** AT LAST-- TO FIND HIMSELF **BOUND** AND **HELPLESS**--

--EVEN AS, NOT FAR OFF, **WOMAN** AND **LION** HALT TO HEAR THAT CLARION CALL.

AND WHO CAN **SAY** IF BOTH HALT FOR THE **SAME** REASON?

IN THE **CAVES** WHICH HONEYCOMB THE CLIFFS ON WHICH ANCIENT ABOMBI WAS BUILT, THE SUMMONS IS ANSWERED-- BY SCREECHING **BABOONS.**

IN THE **JUNGLES** BEYOND, WHERE THE TRUMPET-CALL IS CARRIED BY A STRANGE **AMPLIFICATION** PRODUCED BY THE TWISTING CAVERNS, **OTHER** CREATURES RESPOND IN MUCH THE SAME WAY.

EVEN THICK-SKINNED **CROCODILES** SLITHER FORTH FROM THE RIVERS NEARBY, TO CRAWL WITH EERIE AWKWARD DETERMINATION TOWARD THE **ROCK OF ABOMBI.**

BY TWOS, OR TENS, OR TWELVES, OR EVEN **GREATER** NUMBERS THEY COME...

AND **ALL** WHO SCURRY THITHER ARE **PREDATORS** OF A SORT-- BEASTS WHICH FEED ON OTHER BEASTS, OR ON **MEN**--

--EVEN THOUGH SOME ARE MORE THE **SCAVENGERS** THAN OTHERS.

NOR DO THE **NIGHT SKIES** THEMSELVES FAIL TO GIVE UP THEIR MORE **FOREBODING** INHABITANTS.

AND, **ALL** MOVE WITH RELENTLESS TREAD OR FLURRY--

"Know, O prince, that between the years when the oceans drank Atlantis and the gleaming cities, and the rise of the sons of Aryas, there was an Age undreamed of, when shining kingdoms lay spread across the world like blue mantles beneath the stars.
"Hither came Conan, the Cimmerian, black-haired, sullen-eyed, sword in hand, a thief, a reaver, a slayer, with gigantic melancholies and gigantic mirth, to tread the jeweled thrones of the Earth under his sandaled feet."
—*The Nemedian Chronicles.*

STan Lee PRESENTS: CONAN THE BARBARIAN.

The LONG NIGHT of FANG and TALON! PART TWO

IN THE MIRRORS OF KHARAM-AKKAD, ONCE A WIZARD IN THRICE-DOOMED MAKKALET-- OR IN THE TIME-LOST CLIFF-CITY CALLED ABOMBI-- SOME IMAGES ARE WORTH THE REPEATING

--TILL THERE BE *NAUGHT REMAINING* OF AMRA BUT *FANG-MARKED BONES!*

CROM'S DEVILS!

NO, MOTTLED ONE!

SOON, SOON, I'LL UNLEASH YOU, TO JOIN IN THE *FEAST* OF THE *BLOOD-MOON*--

RRRRR

THE CURSE OF THE TIGHTLY BOUND CONAN, HOWEVER, IS DIRECTED NOT AT THE *LEOPARD* CLAWING THE AIR BEFORE HIM -- OR EVEN AT *AJAGA*, KNOWN AS THE *BEAST-KING*--

ROY THOMAS WRITER/EDITOR

JOHN BUSCEMA & ERNIE CHAN ILLUSTRATORS

TOM ORZECHOWSKI, *letterer*

JIM SHOOTER CONSULTING EDITOR

FEATURING CHARACTERS CREATED BY ROBERT E. HOWARD

LG347

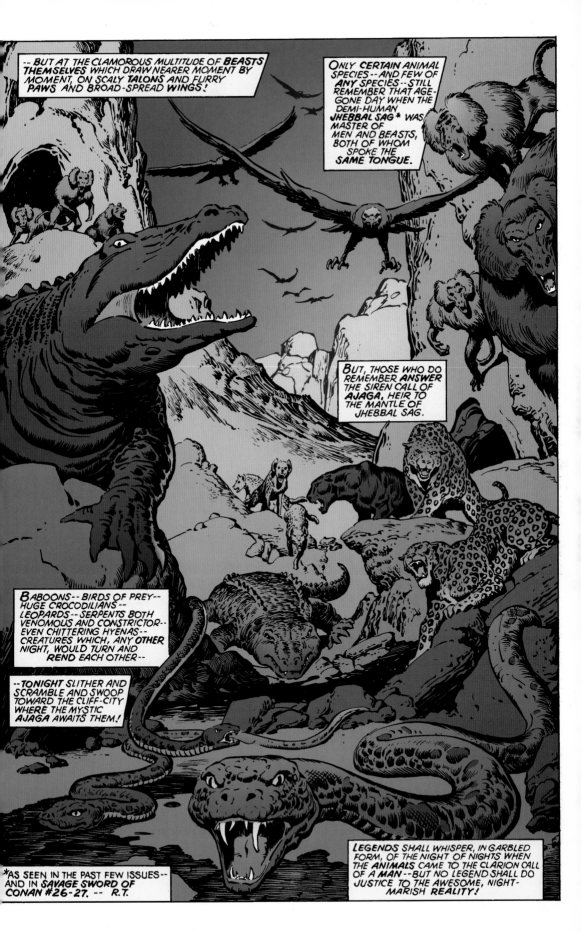

-- BUT AT THE CLAMOROUS MULTITUDE OF *BEASTS* THEMSELVES WHICH DRAW NEARER MOMENT BY MOMENT, ON SCALY *TALONS* AND FURRY *PAWS* AND BROAD-SPREAD *WINGS!*

ONLY *CERTAIN ANIMAL* SPECIES -- AND FEW OF *ANY SPECIES* -- STILL REMEMBER THAT AGE-GONE DAY WHEN THE DEMI-HUMAN *JHEBBAL SAG* * WAS MASTER OF MEN AND BEASTS, BOTH OF WHOM SPOKE THE *SAME TONGUE.*

BUT, THOSE WHO DO REMEMBER *ANSWER* THE SIREN CALL OF *AJAGA*, HEIR TO THE MANTLE OF *JHEBBAL SAG.*

BABOONS -- BIRDS OF PREY -- HUGE *CROCODILIANS* -- *LEOPARDS* -- SERPENTS BOTH VENOMOUS AND CONSTRICTOR -- EVEN CHITTERING *HYENAS* -- CREATURES WHICH, ANY *OTHER* NIGHT, WOULD TURN AND *REND EACH OTHER* --

-- TONIGHT SLITHER AND SCRAMBLE AND SWOOP TOWARD THE CLIFF-CITY WHERE THE MYSTIC *AJAGA* AWAITS THEM!

*AS SEEN IN THE PAST FEW ISSUES -- AND IN *SAVAGE SWORD OF CONAN* #26-27. -- R.T.

LEGENDS SHALL WHISPER, IN GARBLED FORM, OF THE NIGHT OF NIGHTS WHEN THE *ANIMALS* CAME TO THE CLARION CALL OF *A MAN* -- BUT NO LEGEND SHALL DO JUSTICE TO THE AWESOME, NIGHT-MARISH *REALITY!*

AND, ON HIS ROCK-CARVED STAGE, AJAGA OF ABOMBI STRUTS BEFORE HIS BESTIAL AND HUMAN MINIONS...

YOU AND THAT SHE-DEVIL BÊLIT THOUGHT TO RETURN TO RULE THE BLACK COAST AS BEFORE, AMRA.

BUT, YOU RECKONED WITHOUT THE POWER OF AJAGA!

POWER? POWER THAT HIDES BEHIND DUMB BRUTES!

RELEASE ME, AND PUT A SWORD IN MY HAND--AND I'LL TAKE ON YOU AND YOUR LEOPARD!

BUT, EVEN AJAGA IS NOT THAT INSANE.

FROM OVERHEAD NOW, SAFE BEHIND THE STRANGE SYMBOL OF JHEBBAL SAG WHICH THEIR MASTER HAS DRAWN IN THE ROCK AND DUST, HIS FOLLOWERS WATCH IN SILENT AWE--

--AND AMONG THEM, NONE MORE ANXIOUSLY THAN THE TWO BROTHERS, KRATO AND BEEYA, THE BEAST-KING'S BEPLUMED SUB-CHIEFS--

--AS, ONCE AGAIN, AJAGA UTTERS WEIRD AND INHUMAN CRIES WHICH REVERBERATE THROUGHOUT THE CLIFFS AND EVEN THE JUNGLE BEYOND!

AT HIS HEELS, THE GREAT PANTHER SNARLS, YET SEEMS TO UNDERSTAND--

GRARRR

--AS, NOT FAR DISTANT, THE FOUR-FOOTED ONES AND THE LEGLESS ONES INCREASE THEIR PACE, IN A PHANTASMAGORICAL PARADE.

NOW, THEY GATHER, SUCH OF THEM AS HAVE HEARD AND HEEDED THE SUMMONS, ON THE FLAT, STONY AREA AROUND *AJAGA...*

NOR CAN THE LISTENING *MEN* TELL WHICH OF THE HARSH, CO-MINGLING SOUNDS *BELOW* COME TRULY FROM THE THROATS OF BEASTS...

...AND WHICH FROM THAT OF *AJAGA* HIMSELF!

YET, EVEN THE *DULLEST* OF THE SAVAGES CAN SENSE THAT THE SHUFFLING CREATURES *COMPREHEND* THEIR HUMAN MASTER, WHO HAS SPOKEN WITH THE *VOICE OF JHEBBAL SAG* SINCE HE FIRST FELL INTO A MADMAN'S TRANCE...

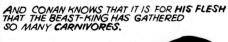

AND CONAN KNOWS THAT IT IS FOR *HIS FLESH* THAT THE BEAST-KING HAS GATHERED SO MANY *CARNIVORES.*

EVEN THE GREAT *BLACK LION SHOLO,* WHICH *REVERES AMRA,* COULD NOT HELP HIM AGAINST *ALL OF THEM.*

HE ONLY THANKS *CROM* THAT *BÉLIT,* AT LEAST, SEEMS TO HAVE ESCAPED... FOR THE MOMENT!

NOW, LET THE *BLOODMOON RITUAL* BEGIN!

HERETOFORE, I HAVE SACRIFICED *WOMEN* WHO PLEASED ME NOT.

THIS NIGHT, MY BEASTS SHALL HAVE THE MIGHTY-THEWED ONE WHO CALLS HIM-SELF -- A *LION!*

WE SHALL SEE IF HE *ROARS* BEFORE HE *DIES--!*

--BÊLIT MUST **STRIKE!**

RRARR

THE CORSAIR QUEEN SCARCELY NOTICES THAT, WITH A RESOUNDING *ROAR*, THE GREAT LION LEAPS *BESIDE* HER, NOT *AT* HER, SO INTENT IS SHE ON REACHING HER *HUMAN* TARGET FAR BELOW.

AND, SMITE HIM SHE *DOES*-- HURTLING THE BEAST- KING

=MMMFF!=

UNNH

--HIS PANTHER-COWLED *HEAD* SMASHING AGAINST A JAGGED-EDGED *ROCK* AS HE TOPPLES HEADLONG!

NEXT MOMENT, HOWEVER, THE LION STOPS SHORT-- FOR, HE HAS LANDED ON THE FAR SIDE OF THE ARCANE AND OMNISCIENT SIGN OF JHEBBAL SAG--

--THAT SIGN WHICH NO *ANIMAL* MAY PASS!

BÊLIT! HOW--?

SHOLO! COME! HERE'S *AMRA!*

DAMN THAT CAT! *WHY* DOESN'T HE--?

KRATO-- BEEYA! *SHOULD* WE--?

FOOLS! SEE HOW EVEN THE *BLACK LION* FEARS THE SYMBOL GREAT AJAGA DREW!

SLAY BOTH BÊLIT AND AMRA-- FOR THE SAKE OF THE *FALLEN MASTER!*

GET *OUT* OF HERE, WOMAN! YOU'LL NEVER GET ME *FREE* IN TIME!

SORRY, BUT I DON'T SEEM TO BE *HEARING* SO WELL TONIGHT.

SON OF A BRYTHUNIAN! YOU MADE IT, AT *THAT!*

I'LL GET THIS OTHER BOND.

BUT-- WHY NO MORE *KUSHITE SPEARS* WHIZZING THROUGH THE AIR?

TURN YOUR HEAD AND YOU'LL *SEE!*

THEY'VE GOT US *SURROUNDED*-- AND THEY'RE COMING IN FOR THE *KILL!*

THEN WE'LL DIE *TOGETHER*-- NOT THE *WORST* WAY TO GO THAT I CAN THINK OF!

BUT, WHAT OF *AJAGA* AND HIS *BEASTS?*

HAH! THERE THEY ARE!

THE ANIMALS ARE *CONFUSED* BY HIS *SILENCE!* HIS *SPELL* OVER THEM MUST BE *FADING* WITH EACH SECOND!

RRR

SSSS

CHREE

WELL, WE'LL JUST SEE IF WE CAN'T *HELP THINGS ALONG* A BIT--

--BY *WASHING AWAY* MUCH OF THE SO-CALLED *SIGN OF JHEBBAL SAG!*

AT LEAST, NOW AJAGA'S *WARRIORS* CAN'T HURL THEIR SPEARS FROM A *SAFE HAVEN!*

AND, AS EVEN THAT PORTION OF THE *ARCANE SYMBOL* WHICH WAS MOSTLY CARVED ONLY IN *DUST* VANISHES *FOREVER--*

--AJAGA HIMSELF AWAKENS, TO FIND HIMSELF SURROUNDED BY *WILD THINGS* WHICH SNIFF AND PAW THE DIRT-COVERED ROCK--

WHAT THE DEVIL--?

AWAY, YE BEASTS!

RRRR

KEEP AWAY FROM ME!

THEY MERELY MOVE *CLOSER*... MANY WITH *FANGS* BARED.

KEEP BACK! DON'T YOU *UNDERSTAND* YOUR MASTER???

DESPERATELY, HE TRIES TO SPEAK IN THE *TONGUE OF BEASTS* --

CHRR

BUT, HIS HEAD STILL *THROBBING* MADLY, HE HAS *FORGOTTEN HOW*-- AND ONLY UNINTELLIGIBLE, HALF-HUMAN *SPUTTERINGS* COME FORTH...!

IT IS HIS OWN SPOTTED FAMILIAR WHICH BREAKS THE GRIM TABLEAU OF MAN AND ANIMALS WITH A SUDDEN LEAP--!

GRARR

NO! S-STAY BACK!!

I AM AJAGA! I AM THE BEAST-KING--!

YET, TO THE **SCALED** AND **PINIONED** AND **FURRY** ONES WHO NOW ATTACK, THIS IS **NOT** THE DEMI-SPIRIT THAT CALLED THEM FORTH FROM RIVER AND SKY AND JUNGLE--

SNARRL

SHRR

YIP YIP

--BUT MERELY A CRINGING **MANLING** FOR WHOM THEY EACH FEEL A MOMENTARY, ALL-CONSUMING **HATRED** AS STRONG AS THEIR EARLIER **ATTRACTION!**

ABOUT **ONE** THING, AT LEAST, AJAGA WAS **CORRECT**--

THE **FEAST** OF THE **BLOODMOON** WILL BE HELD, INDEED, THIS NIGHT.

THEN, THEIR **COMMON PREY** DISPOSED OF, THE MYRIAD BEASTS ABRUPTLY REVERT **TOTALLY** TO THEIR FORMER SELVES--

-- FALLING UPON **EACH OTHER** WITH A FIERCENESS THAT RIVALS EVEN THEIR ASSAULT ON THE LATE, UNLAMENTED **AJAGA!**

TEETH AND **TALONS** AND **COILS** INTERMINGLE VIOLENTLY, IN A WHIRLING MIASMA OF **BLOOD** AND **ENTRAILS**--

AND CONAN, **ASTONISHED**, ALMOST WISHES HE'D NOT WASHED AWAY SO MUCH OF THE **MAGIC** SYMBOL, AFTER ALL!

HE AND HIS MATE STILL STAND READY TO **PERISH**, IF NEED BE, BEFORE THE SPEARS OF **AJAGA'S** MINIONS...

THEY, HOWEVER, STAND GAZING IN SUCH STUPEFIED **AMAZEMENT** AT THE BATTLING, WRITHING BEASTS, THAT THEY ARE FORGETFUL OF THE **CORSAIRS** IN THEIR MIDST--

-- UNTIL ONE OF THE KUSHITES BLUNDERS TOO NEAR *BÊLIT*, WHO TAKES HIS ACTION AS A THREAT-- AND RESPONDS.

YYYY

THEN, THE *HUMAN BATTLE* IS JOINED FOR REAL-- EVEN AMID THE *SLAUGHTER OF THE BEASTS!*

THE ERSTWHILE *LEOPARD-FAMILIAR*, HOWEVER, STILL RETAINS MENTAL IMAGES OF THE *TWO-LEGGED* ONES IT HAD FOUGHT BEFORE--

--INCLUDING THE DARK-TRESSED *SHE-PIRATE* WHO STABS, WITH BACK TURNED, AT *HUMAN* FOES.

BUT, BEFORE IT CAN *LEAP*--

SHOLO!

RARRG

RRRR

--THE *BLACK LION* IS THERE!

AND *BÊLIT* IS GLAD THAT *ONE* CARNIVORE, AT LEAST, HAS NOT FORGOTTEN ENTIRELY ITS *HUMAN CONNECTIONS.*

THE **OTHER** PREDATORS, HOWEVER, HAVE FORGOTTEN EVERYTHING BUT THE **FEAR AND LOATHING** THEY FEEL IN THE PRESENCE OF THEIR NATURAL AND UNNATURAL FOES.

EACH WOULD PREFER TO **FLEE,** GIVEN ITS CHOICE-- BUT THE **BLOOD-MADNESS** IS UPON MANY OF THEM NOW--

AND EACH CREATURE FEELS IT MUST **FIGHT--** OR ELSE BE **SLAIN,** IF IT TURNS ITS BACK!

ALREADY, MANY OF THOSE WHO ANSWERED THE **HORN OF AJAGA,** AND WHO RESPONDED TO THE **TONGUE OF JHEBBAL SAG,** WILL ANSWER NO MORE TO THE CALL OF THE WILD...

AS, NEARBY...

SLAY HIM, BEEYA! AMRA **MUST NOT LIVE!**

AYE! HE MUST **PERISH--** FOR KILLING AJAGA'S DREAMS OF **CONQUEST!**

SO! YOU **TWO** ARE **AGREED,** THEN!

WELL, NO ONE EVER ASKED **ME** ABOUT IT!

WITH HIS HEADLONG LEAP, CONAN **BOWLS** OVER ONE OF THE CHIEFTAIN BROTHERS-- BUT HE HIMSELF IS HURLED TO THE **GROUND** IN THE PROCESS--

AND, BEFORE EVEN HE CAN RISE--!

NOW, YOU DIE-- AT THE HAND OF KRATO!

RRAWRR

MOTHER OF MITRA!

WITH A REACTION WHICH IS PURE INSTINCT, THE FRIGHT-FILLED SUB-CHIEF HOLDS UP HIS SPEAR-- BRACED, BY SHEER ACCIDENT, AGAINST A MIGHTY BOULDER BEHIND HIM.

THE BLACK LION'S SPRING SENDS THE SHAFT OF THE WEAPON CLEAR THROUGH ITS GREAT BODY--

-- EVEN AS ITS OWN WIDE-SPREAD JAWS CLAMP DOWN IN DEATH-AGONY ON WHAT WAS ONCE A HUMAN FACE.

YYAAAA*

JUST SO SWIFTLY... IT IS OVER.

SHOLO...!

KRATO--!

EACH OF US MOURNS THE DEATHS ONLY OF THOSE WE KNOW... AND WE RESIGN TO ETERNAL OBLIVION ALL OTHER DEATHS, AS IF THEY NEVER HAPPENED AT ALL.

ONLY THUS, DOUBTLESS, CAN WE SURVIVE OUR LIFETIMES... WITHOUT GOING MAD.

THE *ANIMALS,* TOO, HAVE EXPENDED ALL THEIR *SAVAGE ENERGIES...*

... AND THOSE WHICH STILL *LIVE* NOW STUMBLE, CRAWL, OR LOPE BACK TOWARD THEIR *NATURAL HABITATS.*

WITHIN MOMENTS, THE CARVEN STAGE IS VIRTUALLY *EMPTY* OF *LIVING BEASTS...*

... A FACT NOT LOST ON *BEEYA,* THE SURVIVING SUB-CHIEF:

HE SEES THAT THE *WARRIORS,* TOO, ARE BEGINNING TO *SCATTER,* HAVING NO MORE TASTE FOR *BATTLE* NOW THAT THEIR *MASTER* IS DEAD.

YET, WHERE *ONE* MASTER HAS FALLEN... CANNOT *ANOTHER ARISE?*

HOLD, *DOGS!* DO NOT *FLEE* LIKE *CRAVEN JACKALS!*

DAMN HIS PLUMED SKULL! I HOPED WE WERE *OUT OF THE FOREST,* AT LAST!

NOT WHILE THERE IS *ABANDONED POWER* TO BE GRASPED IN *GREEDY* HANDS!

NOR CAN *WE* FLEE -- FOR FEAR OF RUNNING INTO THE RETREATING *MEAT-EATERS* IN DARKNESS.

STAND *READY* TO FIGHT *ANEW!*

COME, *WARRIORS!* LET US *SLAY AMRA* AND *BÊLIT!*

THEN, WE SHALL *REIGN SUPREME* ON THE BLACK COAST -- *AJAGA* OR *NO AJAGA!*

KILL *THEM!*

IF THE KUSHITES HOPE TO SPEAR FLEEING FOES IN THE *BACK*, HOWEVER, THEY SOON LEARN THE *FOLLY* OF THOSE HOPES--

HAAAAAHHH!

--AS CONAN AND HIS SNARLING MATE *RUSH TOWARD* THEM INSTEAD, EACH CARRYING MORE THAN A SINGLE FOEMAN BACKWARD WITH THE *SHEER FURY* OF THE CHARGE!

STILL, NOT FOR *LONG* CAN THE EMBATTLED PAIR HOPE TO ENDURE AGAINST SUCH SUPERIOR NUMBERS, IF THE BLACK WARRIORS KEEP *STOMACH* FOR THE FIGHT-- AS IT SEEMS THEY *WILL.*

CONAN! SELL YOUR LIFE *DEARLY,* MY LOVER!

THEY'LL PAY FOR IT IN *BLOOD* AND SHATTERED *BONES,* WOMAN!

STILL, AT *WHATEVER* COST, IT APPEARS THE PURCHASE *WILL* BE MADE--

--TILL, WITHOUT WARNING--!

WHAT IN ISHTAR'S NAME--?

M'GORA-- AND THE BLACK CORSAIRS!

WE COME, GODDESS!

AND *THIS* TIME, BOTH SHEER NUMBERS AND FIGHTING PROWESS FAVOR THE *PIRATES!*

IT TAKES BUT A FEW MINUTES FOR *BEEYA* TO DISCERN WHICH WAY THE *WINDS OF CHANCE* NOW BLOW...

... AS HE SEES THOSE HE'D HOPED TO FORGE INTO A *MIGHTY ARMY* GO DOWN LIKE CHAFF BEFORE THE ATTACK OF THE *CORSAIRS.*

LOOKING UP FROM THE SLAUGHTER, CONAN BEHOLDS THE FLEEING FORM...

HOLD, BEEYA! YOU WANTED *VENGEANCE* FOR THE DEATH OF YOUR *BROTHER!*

FACE ME-- AND WE'LL SOON SEE *WHO* AVENGES *WHAT!*

NAY! YOU ARE *MIGHTIER* WITH SWORD AND SPEAR THAN I -- I KNOW THAT--

YET, IT *WAS* YOU, MORE THAN ANY *LION,* WHO *SLEW MY BROTHER!*

AND I'LL *HAVE* MY REVENGE, ONE DAY-- IF IT TAKES A *LIFETIME!* *

THEN... HE IS GONE, INTO THE *DARKNESS.*

AMRA! GODDESS! ALL AJAGA'S MEN SEEM TO BE *DEAD--* OR ELSE *GONE,* AT LEAST!

SHALL WE *PURSUE* THE PLUMED ONE, INTO THE *CAVES ABOVE?*

NO, M'GORA...

*ACTUALLY, BEEYA'S SECOND AND FINAL ATTEMPT ON CONAN'S LIFE OCCURRED SOME *TWO DECADES* LATER -- AS SEEN IN *"THE SCARLET CITADEL,"* IN *SAVAGE SWORD* #30.--R.

DESPITE HIS THREAT OF REVENGE, IT'S DOUBTFUL ANY OF US WILL EVER *LAY EYES* ON BEEYA AGAIN.

YOUR WORD IS OUR *COMMAND,* O AMRA.

RATHER, YOURS SHOULD BE *OURS,* WARRIOR.

IF NOT FOR YOU, WE'D BOTH RESIDE NOW IN THE *BELLIES OF BEASTS,* eh, MY LOVER?

CONAN DOES NOT ANSWER.

HIS MATE'S WORDS HAVE REMINDED HIM, TO HIS SORROW...

...OF THAT GREAT, SHAGGY FORM LYING NEARBY, PIERCED BY A SAVAGE'S SPEAR.

SHOLO...!

BUT, THE BLACK LION IS BEYOND ALL HELP.

SWIFTLY, CONAN RAISES A ROCK CAIRN OVER HIS REMAINS...

...A FINAL HOMAGE FROM ONE ELEMENTAL FORCE... TO ANOTHER.

HE SERVED YOU *WELL,* CONAN... AMRA.

AYE, BÊLIT-- HE SERVED *TWO* AMRAS WELL.

IT'S NOT WITHIN MY POWER TO KNOW *WHY,* PRECISELY... BUT ANY TIME OUR SHIP *PASSES* THE CLIFFS OF ABOMBI, FROM THIS DAY FORWARD...

...I'LL SHOOT AN *ARROW* INTO THE SKY, TO SALUTE AN *ANIMAL* NOBLER BY FAR THAN MOST *MEN* I'VE KNOWN.

THEN, AFTER FREEING SEVERAL CORSAIRS CAPTURED EARLIER WITH BÊLIT...

AJAGA'S *CAPTIVE BRIDES* ARE KEPT IN HERE, YOU SAY?

AYE.

AS WAS *I*, TILL SHOLO SET ME FREE.

LOOK! IT IS THE *DAUGHTER OF THE DEATH-GODDESS*, COME BACK TO SAVE US!

F-FORGIVE US, O BÊLIT, FOR FEARING TO *ACT* WITH YOU!

SAY NO MORE OF IT.

SOME ARE *BORN* TO FIGHT-- OTHERS *NOT*.

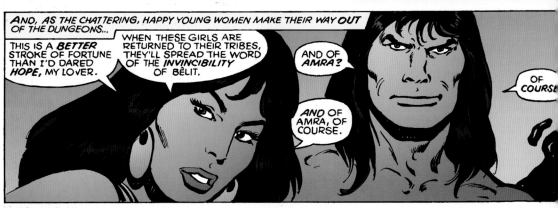

AND, AS THE CHATTERING, HAPPY YOUNG WOMEN MAKE THEIR WAY *OUT* OF THE DUNGEONS...

THIS IS A *BETTER* STROKE OF FORTUNE THAN I'D DARED *HOPE*, MY LOVER.

WHEN THESE GIRLS ARE RETURNED TO THEIR TRIBES, THEY'LL SPREAD THE WORD OF THE *INVINCIBILITY* OF BÊLIT.

AND OF *AMRA*?

AND OF AMRA, OF COURSE.

OF COURSE!

SOON, ITS HOLD HEAVY WITH THE *TRIBUTE* EXACTED BY AJAGA AND HIS NOW-SCATTERED MINIONS, THE *TIGRESS* PUTS OUT TO SEA AGAIN...

... LEAVING *NO LIVING THING* IN AGE-OLD ABOMBI, SAVE THE LIZARD AND AN OCCASIONAL SEA-CRAB.

BUT *ONCE*, FOR ONE DARK MOMENT, ABOMBI AND ITS *BEAST-KING* LOOKED TO HOLD THE WHOLE *BLACK COAST* IN THRALL... ONLY TO PASS FROM THE SCENE, AND INTO THE FRAGILE MEMORY OF MAN.

THERE IS A LESSON THERE FOR ALL... AYE, EVEN FOR CONAN... AND FOR THE SHE-PIRATE CALLED BÊLIT...!

NEXT SEA-WOMAN!

"Know, O prince, that between the years when the oceans drank Atlantis and the gleaming cities, and the rise of the sons of Aryas, there was an Age undreamed of, when shining kingdoms lay spread across the world like blue mantles beneath the stars.

"Hither came Conan, the Cimmerian, black-haired, sullen-eyed, sword in hand, a thief, a reaver, a slayer, with gigantic melancholies and gigantic mirth, to tread the jeweled thrones of the Earth under his sandaled feet."

—The Nemedian Chronicles.

STAN LEE PRESENTS: CONAN THE BARBARIAN ®

SEA-WOMAN!

JUST AFTER DAWN, UPON THE WESTERN OCEAN--

AMRA! LOOK YOU TO STARBOARD-- AND TELL AJAGA HIS EYES ARE DECEIVING HIM!

EH? NOW WHAT KIND OF CRY IS THAT FROM A LOOKOUT, CORSAIR?

IF THERE'S A MERCHANT SHIP RIPE FOR LOOTING, JUST SAY--

--SO.

HOLY MOTHER OF MITRA!

ROY THOMAS
WRITER/EDITOR

JOHN BUSCEMA & ERNIE CHAN
ILLUSTRATORS

JOE ROSEN
LETTERER

JIM SHOOTER
CONSULTING EDITOR

FEATURING CHARACTERS AND CONCEPTS CREATED BY ROBERT E. HOWARD
(POEM "SEA-WOMAN" COPYRIGHT © 1970 BY GLENN LORD)

IN A MOMENT, **ALL** EYES OF THOSE ABOARD THE SEA-ROVING TIGRESS ARE TURNED IN THE DIRECTION INDICATE BY AJAGA'S SHOUT:

THOSE OF **BÊLIT**, SHEMITISH-BORN CAPTAIN OF THE PIRATE VESSEL...

...OF **M'GORA**, FIRST OF HER BLACK-CORSAIR SUB-CHIEFS...

...OF **N'YAGA**, THE OLD SHAMAN WHO IS BÊLIT'S MENTOR...

...AND OF COURSE, THOSE OF **CONAN**, ALSO CALLED **AMRA**.

AND THAT WHICH THEY NOW **BEHOLD** LEAVES THEM EACH **SPEECHLESS** FOR A LONG, LINGERING MOMENT--

A **WOMAN**, AZURE OF FLESH, AND WITH FREE-FLOWING HAIR THE COLOR OF SOME RADIANT TYPE OF SEAWEED...

...A WOMAN, YOUNG AND FAIR OF FACE AND FORM, WHO MUST BY ALL RIGHTS HAVE BEEN LOST OFF SOME TEMPEST-TOSSED AND PIRATE-SUNK **SHIP**...

...YET WHO **STANDS**, SILENT AND NEARLY UN-MOVING AS A STATUE, ATOP WHAT SEEMS A HUGE, BOBBING **LILY PAD**...A THING WHICH SEEMS A POOR LIFE-BOAT INDEED!

I'LL HAVE TO TENDER MY APOLOGIES TO OUR HAWK-EYED LOOKOUT, IT SEEMS.

SMALL WONDER HE THOUGHT HIS EYES PLAYED *TRICKS* ON HIM!

PERHAPS THE TROPICAL SUN HAS GOT TO *ALL* OF US--

FOR, SURELY THE SHEER MOTION OF THE *WAVES* WOULD TOSS THE WOMAN TO HER *KNEES*-- YET SHE *STANDS!*

I SAY SHE'S SOME KIND OF *SEA-WITCH*-- AND I SAY WE *LET HER BE!*

NOR IS IT MERELY HER USUAL POS-SESSIVE JEALOUS SPIRIT WHICH SPURS BÊLIT'S THOUGHTS...

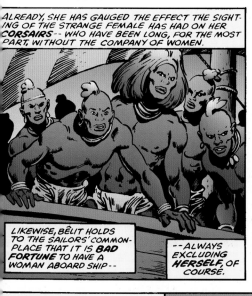

ALREADY, SHE HAS GAUGED THE EFFECT THE SIGHT-ING OF THE STRANGE FEMALE HAS HAD ON HER *CORSAIRS*-- WHO HAVE BEEN LONG, FOR THE MOST PART, WITHOUT THE COMPANY OF WOMEN.

LIKEWISE, BÊLIT HOLDS TO THE SAILORS' COMMON-PLACE THAT IT IS *BAD FORTUNE* TO HAVE A WOMAN ABOARD SHIP--

--ALWAYS EXCLUDING *HERSELF*, OF COURSE.

STILL, IT TAKES BUT *ONE MAN* TO DISSUADE HER FROM PASSING THE APPARENT CASTAWAY BY...

I BEG YOU, BRING HER *ABOARD*, GODDESS.

I PROMISE YOU, I WOULD *KNOW* IF SHE MEANT EVIL.... AND ALL MY INSTINCTS TELL ME SHE DOES *NOT*.

ALL RIGHT, N'YAGA, BUT--

LOOK!

AT THEIR CAPTAIN'S CRY, ALL HANDS TURN AGAIN TOWARD THE VISION SOME DISTANCE AWAY...TO WHICH A *NEW* ELEMENT HAS BEEN SUDDENLY ADDED--

THE SINISTER *FIN* OF A GREAT *SHARK*.

WITH STEADY, RELENTLESS SPEED, THE FIN MOVES TOWARD THE FRAIL LILY PAD AND THE WOMAN UPON IT.

FOR LONG SECONDS, SHE SEEMS NOT TO *NOTICE* IT... AS SHE GALES AHEAD AT THE DRIFTING TIGRESS.

THEN, SLOWLY TURNING HER GRAY-BLUE FACE TOWARD IT, SHE OPENS HER *MOUTH* WIDE...

...THOUGH, IF SHE UTTERS A SOUND, THOSE WATCHING DO NOT *HEAR* IT.

AT WHAT SEEMS THE LAST POSSIBLE INSTANT, THE SHARK-FIN *VEERS AWAY* FROM THE GENTLY BOBBING PAD...

...SOON DISAPPEARING UNDERWATER, TO BE SEEN NO MORE.

NEITHER DOES SHE SPEAK TO THE *CORSAIRS* WHO, SOON AFTERWARD, HAUL HER ABOARD THEIR HASTILY DISPATCHED LONGBOAT.

I'VE SEEN SUCH BLANK, STARING LOOKS *BEFORE*, THOUGH MOSTLY FROM *LUNATICS*--OR THOSE WHO'VE GAPED INTO THE *JAWS OF HELL.*

PERHAPS FEAR OF THE *SHARK,* OR OF *DROWNING*--!

PERHAPS.

WHAT THINK *YOU*, SHAMAN?

I...I AM HAVING *DIFFICULTY* THINKING, DAUGHTER OF DERKETA.

PERHAPS. OR ELSE...THE *STRAIN* OF ALL THIS.

I'LL TAKE TO MY *QUARTERS* A WHILE...

EH? WHAT'S WRONG, MY *MENTOR*? A RECURRENCE OF YOUR RECENT *ILLNESS*?

N'YAGA *IS* OLD, BÊLIT REMINDS HERSELF, AND *YET...!*

HER THOUGHTS ARE INTERRUPTED AS THE AGED WITCH-DOCTOR VANISHES BELOW-DECKS...AND THE GIRL ABRUPTLY *RISES UP* WITH RENEWED VIGOR.

SHE OPENS HER LIPS...BUT *NO WORDS* COME OUT.

SHE IS A *MUTE,* PERHAPS.

OR PERHAPS SIMPLY ACCUSTOMED TO NO *HAVING* TO SPEAK, TO GET WHAT SHE WANTS.

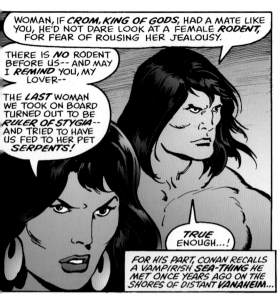

WOMAN, IF *CROM, KING OF GODS*, HAD A MATE LIKE YOU, HE'D NOT DARE LOOK AT A FEMALE *RODENT*, FOR FEAR OF ROUSING HER JEALOUSY.

THERE IS *NO* RODENT BEFORE US-- AND MAY I *REMIND* YOU, MY LOVER--

THE *LAST* WOMAN WE TOOK ON BOARD TURNED OUT TO BE *RULER OF STYGIA*-- AND TRIED TO HAVE US FED TO HER PET *SERPENTS!*

TRUE ENOUGH...!

FOR HIS PART, CONAN RECALLS A VAMPIRISH *SEA-THING* HE MET ONCE YEARS AGO ON THE SHORES OF DISTANT *VANAHEIM*...

BUT, THAT CREATURE HAD TO RETURN TO THE *OCEAN'S DEPTHS* BY DAWN, WHILE THIS DELICATE-APPEARING WENCH SCARCELY SHUNS THE LIGHT OF DAY.

NOR, INCREASINGLY, DO THE CORSAIRS SHUN *HER.*

M'GORA! GET THESE SONS OF THE SILVER ISLES BACK TO *WORK!*

AYE, GODDESS.

WE'RE STILL A *PIRATE SHIP,* NOT A SERVICE FOR *CAST-OFFS!*

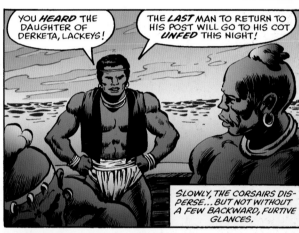

YOU *HEARD* THE DAUGHTER OF DERKETA, LACKEYS!

THE *LAST* MAN TO RETURN TO HIS POST WILL GO TO HIS COT *UNFED* THIS NIGHT!

SLOWLY, THE CORSAIRS DISPERSE...BUT NOT WITHOUT A FEW BACKWARD, FURTIVE GLANCES.

NEXT MORNING, THERE IS LITTLE TIME FOR ANY TO MOON OVER A STRANGE AND SILENT FEMALE...

..AS A *STYGIAN* MERCHANT VESSEL IS SIGHTED...

AND, THOUGH MANNED BY NOT A FEW DUSKY-SKINNED *SOLDIERS,* IT PROVES NO MATCH FOR THE MEN OF THE *TIGRESS,* WHO SWIFTLY OVERPOWER THEM AND SEND BOTH SEAMEN AND SHIP TO THE *BOTTOM.*

EVEN WITH HER THRONE RE-WON AND GIVEN AWAY, BÊLIT HAS *SCANT LOVE* FOR THAT LAND OF SNAKE-WORSHIPERS AND SORCERERS.

THE STYGIAN TURNS OUT TO HAVE BEEN A *RICH* SHIP, FOR ALL ITS MEAGRE DEFENSES...AND GREAT IS THE *LOOT* THEREOF.

ALL OF WHICH GIVES THE SHE-PIRATE A SUDDEN NOTION OF HOW TO **DISTRACT** HER FIERCE CREW FROM THEIR BEAUTEOUS PASSENGER...

YOU FOUGHT **WELL** THIS DAY, MY CORSAIRS.

WHY DON'T YOU **DIVIDE** THIS CATCH BETWEEN YOU, EACH MAN EQUALLY?

SHE DOES **NOT** HAVE TO REPEAT HERSELF.

STILL, HER SCHEME IS FAR FROM AN UNQUALIFIED **SUCCESS**...

...AS **B'TUMI**, ONE OF THOSE WHO FIRST PULLED THE SILENT WOMAN FROM THE SEA, GOES TO HER, AND...

YOU WOULD **LIKE** THIS PRETTY THING, YES?

SHE SMILES... AND HE GIVES IT TO HER WITHOUT A SECOND THOUGHT.

HE IS NEITHER SMARTER NOR MORE FOOLISH THAN OTHER MEN, IN OTHER TIMES.

YET, EVEN AS HE TURNS HIS BACK...

WHAT THE **DEVIL**--?

THAT NECKLACE IS STILL **WARM** FROM B'TUMI'S HAND...AND YOU'RE OFFERING IT TO **ME**?

I DON'T THINK YOU UNDERSTAND THE **RULES** OF THE GAME, GIRL.

I HOPE I DON'T **OFFEND** YOU, SINCE YOU DON'T SEEM TO KNOW ANY TONGUE I SPEAK, BUT--

NO, THANKS.

WHETHER SHE COMPREHENDS OR NOT, CONAN COULD NOT SAY.

STILL, AS SHE RETURNS TO THE MEN OF THE SOUTHERN ISLES, CONAN SEES THE **DARK RAGE** SEETHING BEHIND HIS MATE'S OBSIDIAN EYES...

...AND FIGURES HE MAY JUST HAVE SAVED THE GIRL'S **LIFE**.

WHILE THE **WOMAN OF AZURE,** FOR HER PART, TURNS MORE OPENLY TO WHAT THE COURTIERS OF AQUILONIA AND NEMEDIA WOULD CALL **FLIRTATION** WITH THE SAVAGE CREWMEN...

...WITH THE NIGH-UNIVERSAL **RESULTS**--

HAH! YOU **SEE,** FRIEND? I THOUGHT SHE **SPURNED** MY GIFT, BUT NOW SHE--

BY AJUJO! OUR GODDESS-CAPTAIN GIVES YOU A FEW BAUBLES--AND THEY GO AT ONCE TO YOUR **HEADS!**

BACK TO YOUR POSTS--

--BEFORE I **STRING YOU UP** WITH YOUR PURLOINED JEWELS!

THAT NIGHT, AS THE FULL MOON GLISTENS LIKE ONE MORE PIRATED GEM ABOVE THE TREASURE CHEST WHICH IS THE SEA...

...A BRONZE-SKINNED **BARBARIAN** WALKS THE DECKS, HIS MIND TROUBLED BY NAME-LESS, HALF-FORMED THOUGHTS.

THE SLIGHTEST **NOISE** BRINGS HIM BACK TO PANTHERISH ALERTNESS...

EH? SO IT'S **YOU,** EH, GIRL?

I'LL SAY THIS-- YOUR SKIN LOOKS MORE **NATURAL** IN THE MOONLIGHT THAN EVER UNDER THE SUN.

BUT WHAT ARE YOU DOING **ABOVE-DECKS** THIS TIME OF NIGHT?

YOU SHOULD BE--

THEN THE GIRL PARTS HER PURPLE **LIPS** ONCE MORE...

AND, THOUGH HE HEARS **NO SOUND,** IT IS AS IF A SENSUOUS, LUST-FUL **SYMPHONY** SUDDENLY SETS HIS BRAIN **AFIRE.**

THOUGH THEY HAVE NOT SO MUCH AS *TOUCHED*, IT TAKES A *TIGERISH* EFFORT FOR CONAN TO TEAR HIMSELF AWAY FROM HER INTENSE GAZE.

NEXT, EVEN AS SHE LOUNGES LANGUOROUSLY AGAINST THE MAINMAST...

...HE RETURNS TO THE CAPTAINS' CABIN.

CONAN... WHAT *IS* IT?

YOU LOOK...SO *STRANGE*, SOMEHOW.

DON'T TALK, WOMAN.

JUST THIS *ONCE*...

...DON'T TALK!

AND SHE *DOESN'T*.

MEANWHILE, A RESTLESS *B'TUMI* HAS RISEN FROM HIS SLEEPLESS COT... FOR IT HAS SUDDENLY OCCURRED TO HIM THAT A WALK ABOVE-DECKS WOULD DO HIM GOOD.

GIRL...?!

I HAD *HOPED* YOU WOULD BE...

YET A *THIRD* TIME, THE GIRL FROM THE SEA OPENS HER MOUTH...

...AND B'TUMI DOES NOT SPEAK AGAIN.

NEXT MORNING...

GODDESS! AMRA! B'TUMI IS MISSING!

WHAT? ARE YOU SURE, MAN?

AYE! WE FOUND ONE OF HIS EARRINGS BY THIS RAILING.

HE MUST HAVE FALLEN OVERBOARD IN THE NIGHT!

YES...YES, I GUESS HE MUST HAVE.

AND THERE ARE OTHERS I'D TOSS OVER AS WELL... IF I FELT THE CORSAIRS WOULD STAND FOR IT.

FROM NOW ON, M'GORA, I WANT NO MAN WALKING THIS DECK ALONE... OR ANY WOMAN, EITHER!

NO LOOTABLE SHIPS OR CONVENIENT PORTS BEING IN SIGHT, M'GORA BUSIES THE EBONY WARRIORS WITH GAMES OF SPEAR AGAINST SPEAR... SINEW AGAINST SINEW.

IT WORKS NO BETTER OR WORSE THAN SUCH TACTICS HAVE EVER WORKED.

THAT NIGHT, IN THE CABIN OF THE AILING SHAMAN...

N'YAGA...?

O MY DEAREST... DEAREST WILIDA... YOUR LIPS ARE AS THE HONEY THE BEES MAKE... AND YOUR--

HE IS DREAMING OF HIS YOUTH...SUCH DREAMS AS HAVE NOT COME TO HIM IN MANY, MANY A DAY.

FOR HOURS, BÊLIT KEEPS SILENT VIGIL BY HER AGED MENTOR'S SIDE.

ALL THAT IS GOOD OR WISE OR GENTLE IN HER NATURE, SHE KNOWS SHE OWES TO THIS NOW-FRAIL OLD MAN, WHO WORKS MIGHTY JUJU...YET NOW MURMURS OF LONG-LOST LOVE IN UNEASY SLEEP.

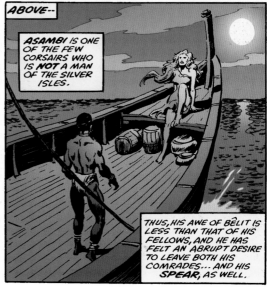

ABOVE--

ASAMBI IS ONE OF THE FEW CORSAIRS WHO IS NOT A MAN OF THE SILVER ISLES.

THUS, HIS AWE OF BÊLIT IS LESS THAN THAT OF HIS FELLOWS, AND HE HAS FELT AN ABRUPT DESIRE TO LEAVE BOTH HIS COMRADES... AND HIS SPEAR, AS WELL.

NOT THAT *EITHER* WOULD BE LIKELY TO DO HIM MUCH GOOD, WHEN THE GIRL OF AZURE ONCE MORE PARTS THOSE LOVELY, UNSPEAKING LIPS.

IT IS AS IF SHE SINGS A *SONG* WHICH NONE BUT *ONE* MAY HEAR, EACH TIME IT'S SUNG...

...A SONG TOO LOVELY, TOO DEEP FOR WORDS *OR* MUSIC.

LIKE A MAN *ENTRANCED,* ASAMBI SEES NOTHING BUT HER...

...AND BECOMES, FOR THE MOMENT, AS MUCH A MUTE AS *SHE.*

WITH A LITHE GESTURE WHICH BELIES HER FORMER APPARENT LANGUID STATE, SHE LEAPS IN ONE FLUID MOTION TO THE *RAILING.*

THEN, WITH A FINAL *GLANCE* AT HER MESMERIZED SLAVE...

...SHE LEAPS *OVERBOARD.*

IT IS AS IF THE LAPPING WAVES *PART* TO RECEIVE HER, SO THAT SHE MAKES NOT SO MUCH AS THE SLIGHTEST SPLASH OR RIPPLE ERE SHE VANISHES BENEATH THE SURFACE...

...LIKE WATER MERGING WITH WATER.

MERE MOMENTS LATER, SHE *REAPPEARS* SOME DISTANCE FROM THE *TIGRESS...RIDING* THE CREST OF A MOONLIT WAVE AS THOUGH IT WERE SOME PROUD WHITE-MANED *STALLION,* AND NOT A THING OF LIQUID AT ALL.

AGAIN SHE SILENTLY "SINGS"...

LOOKING NEITHER TO RIGHT OR LEFT, ASAMBI DIVES *STIFFLY* OVER THE SIDE...

AND SOMEHOW, *HE* MAKES NO SPLASHING SOUND, EITHER, WHEN HE STRIKES THE WATER.

STILL, THERE IS ONE WHO *WATCHES,* FROM LIGHT-DRINKING SHADOWS...

...AS THE BLACK CORSAIR SWIMS WITH MECHANICAL, AWKWARD, YET SOMEHOW POWERFUL STROKES, OUT TOWARD THE WAVE-RIDING *VISION* SOME YARDS FROM THE GENTLY BOBBING SHIP.

WHEN HE REACHES HER, SHE *BENDS DOWN* EVER SO SLOWLY FROM HER WATERY THRONE...

...TO *KISS* HIM.

FOR LONG SECONDS, IT SEEMS *JUST A KISS.*

THEN, SUDDENLY, ASAMBI'S EYES **OPEN WIDE** -- IN THE SHOCK OF RECOGNITION OF STARK **FEAR** AND NAKED **TERROR!**

MMMF

FOR, THOUGH HIS HEAD IS STILL ABOVE THE WATER'S SURFACE, THE WOMAN'S KISS SEEMS TO **ENGULF** HIM, AS IF HE WERE **BELOW** IT...!

REALIZING HIS DANGER AT LAST, HE STRUGGLES TO TEAR HIMSELF **FREE.**

AFTER A MINUTE, HIS STRUGGLES **CEASE...**

...AND THERE IS ONLY A FLOATING EBON **CORPSE,** DROWNED BEFORE EVER IT PASSES FULLY BENEATH THE SURFACE.

NOW, FINALLY, **CONAN** SNAPS HIMSELF OUT OF HIS OWN SPECIAL TRANCE...

WITCH! I KNOW YOU NOW FOR WHAT YOU **ARE** --

-- JUST ANOTHER VARIANT OF THE **SEA-VAMPIRES** I HAVE MET BEFORE!

BY CROM, I'LL ROUSE MY **MEN** AND WE'LL PEPPER THE SEA WITH **SPEARS** UNTIL WE --

AGAIN, THE GIRL OPENS HER MOUTH... AND NOW, FOR THE FIRST TIME, CONAN **HEARS** HER SING... INSIDE HIS **OWN HEAD.**

OR RATHER, IN SOME EERIE WAY, IT IS AS IF IT IS **HE** WHO SINGS TO **HER** --

"The wild sea is beating Against the gray sands-- The woman, the sea-woman, Stretches her hands...

"Her eyes, they are mystic
And cold as the sea...

"With slender white fingers
She beckons to me--

"'There are woods in the sea
Though the leaves are all gray,
The ocean's pale roses
Lift dim in the spray.'

"I follow-- I follow--
The gray sea-gull flies--

"Ah, woman--

"--sea-woman--

"--There's death in your eyes."

YET, THOUGH HIS *DAGGER* IS POISED TO STRIKE AS CONAN DRAWS NEAR HER... IT'S NOT REALLY IN HER SEA-GREEN *EYES* THE DANGER LIES...

...BUT IN THAT *KISS* WHICH DROWNS BOTH BODY AND SOUL.

AS THEY EMBRACE, HE SEES HIMSELF AS HE HAS BEEN IN *TIMES PAST*--

ROISTERING, ROARING, *WENCHING*--

LOCKED IN GRIM BATTLE WITH DUSKY *SORCERERS* AND DEADLY *SERPENTS*--

-- AND WITH THE *ARMIES* OF MANY A NATION, WEST AND EAST!

HE BEHOLDS A WOMAN'S RED-HAIRED *HEAD*-- BUT CAN PLACE NO *NAME* WITH IT...

...SEES *DARKER* HAIR, AND EYES THE COLOR OF *NIGHT*...

...BUT HE CAN-NOT QUITE RE-MEMBER *HER* NAME, EITHER.

NO, NOT...QUITE.

WHAT IS IT, THEN, THAT SUDDENLY BRINGS *BÊLIT* RACING FROM N'YAGA'S SIDE, ONTO THE *DECK*...?

CONAN...?

SEVERAL *BLACK CORSAIRS* SWIFTLY JOIN HER, ROUSED BY THE SOUND OF HER VOICE...

STILL, IT IS *SHE* WHO FIRST BEHOLDS THE *DREAD TABLEAU* SO NEAR AND YET A UNIVERSE AWAY...

CONAN!!

THE SOUND OF THAT VOICE HE KNOWS SO WELL BRINGS HIM *PARTWAY* BACK FROM THE CLOYING, WATERY VOID HE SEEMED ABOUT TO ENTER...BUT *ONLY* PARTWAY.

BÊLIT--?!

IN MITRA'S NAME-- *KEEP CALLING* ME!

THE GIRL HOLDS HIM... AND HER GRIP IS *STRONG*, THOUGH WITHOUT APPARENT EFFORT.

BUT THE QUEEN OF THE BLACK COAST *HEARS* THAT FAINT, FARAWAY CRY...

YES! YES, I'LL *CALL* YOU, CONAN!

COME TO ME, CONAN OF CIMMERIA! COME TO *BÊLIT*, WHO *LOVES* YOU!

FORGOTTEN NOW ARE MYTHS OF *AMRA*, THE LION-MAN, AS SHE CALLS OUT *NOT* TO HER RIGHT HAND... BUT TO HER *HEART.*

CONAN! DON'T LEAVE ME, MY CONAN--!

I-- *WON'T!* I SWEAR TO *CROM*--

-- I *WON'T!!*

SOMEHOW, THE GIRL'S HOLD SEEMS *WEAKER* NOW... FAILING WITH EACH DESPERATE *OUT-CRY* FROM THE SHEMITISH SHE-PIRATE...

...THOUGH HE WISHES HE COULD *STAB* HER AS HE PULLS HER ROUGHLY OFF HER WATERY PERCH!

HE CAN'T.

WELL, GIRL-- OR *THING FROM HELL*-- IF *I* CAN'T SLAY YOU AS YOU DESERVE--

--MILADY *BÊLIT* WILL HARDLY BE SO *SQUEAMISH!*

M'GORA! AJONGA! DON'T JUST STAND THERE AS IF *HYPNOTIZED!*

GET A *LINE* TO TOSS HIM, THAT HE MAY BE HAULED ABOARD!

THEN, AS HER MEN *RACE* TO DO HER BIDDING, HER *CALL* FLOATS ONCE MORE OVER THE SOMBRE *WAVES* WHICH SEEM SOMEHOW TO *CHURN* MORE THAN BEFORE, AS IF IN UNHOLY AGITATION.

ONCE, TWICE PERHAPS, CONAN *HESITATES*...BUT ALWAYS HE CONTINUES ON AGAIN, TOWARD THE SOUND OF BÊLIT'S *VOICE*...

...TILL AT LENGTH IT LEADS HIM UP A *ROPE* HURLED OVER THE SHIP'S DARK SIDE.

YET, AS HE PULLS HIMSELF AND HIS WEIRD PRIZE ABOARD...

WELL? WHAT'S WRONG? WHAT ARE YOU ALL *GAPING* AT?

SURELY YOU'RE *USED*, BY NOW, TO THE SIGHT OF--

--A BLUE-SKINNED GIRL.

SEAWEED.

HIS HAND, WHICH NEVER RELINQUISHED ITS STEELY GRASP ON THE SEA-WOMAN'S *HAIR*, NOW HOLDS ONLY SEAWEED.

LOOKING OUT ACROSS THE OCEAN, HE SEEMS TO HEAR HER *SILENT SONG* AGAIN...

"There are woods in the sea Though the leaves are all gray..."

THEN, A *SOFT HAND* UPON HIS SHOULDER...

...AND THE VOICE IS HEARD NO MORE, EITHER WITHIN OR WITHOUT HIS BRAIN.

CONAN... MY LOVER...

NOT JUST YOUR *LOVER*, BÊLIT...

...BUT YOUR *LOVE*.

AND THE *TIGRESS* SAILS ON, LIKE A VAGRANT WIND...!

NEXT ISSUE: **THE CRAB-THINGS THAT WALK LIKE MEN!**

"Know, O prince, that between the years when the oceans drank Atlantis and the gleaming cities, and the rise of the sons of Aryas, there was an Age undreamed of, when shining kingdoms lay spread across the world like blue mantles beneath the stars.
"Hither came Conan, the Cimmerian, black-haired, sullen-eyed, sword in hand, a thief, a reaver, a slayer, with gigantic melancholies and gigantic mirth, to tread the jeweled thrones of the Earth under his sandaled feet."
—The Nemedian Chronicles.

STAN LEE PRESENTS: CONAN THE BARBARIAN

DEVIL-CRABS OF THE DARK CLIFFS!

NIGHT AND DAY THE *JUNGLE TOM-TOMS* BEAT, TELLING ALL WHO LISTEN THAT *BÊLIT* AND HER *MATE* HAVE RETURNED TO THE COAST OF KUSH AND POINTS SOUTH.

THEY ALSO TELL OF *AMRA,* THE DARK-MANED MAN OF IRON WHOSE WRATH IS THAT OF A WOUNDED LION.

SKY-OBSCURING SMOKE RISES FROM THE HUNGRY *FLAMES* WHICH DEVOUR THE VILLAGES WHICH OP-POSE HER RESTORED RULE-- WHILE THOSE WHICH PAY HER TRIBUTE *PROSPER* BEYOND THEIR EARLIER DREAMS.

ROY *THOMAS* * JOHN *BUSCEMA* & ERNIE *CHAN*
ARTISTS

JOE ROSEN
LETTERER

JIM SHOOTER, CONSULTING EDITOR

AND, HEEDLESS AS AN ERRANT WIND, THE *TIGRESS* CRUISES THE SOUTHERN COASTS, DISPENSING DEATH... AND *DESTINY...!*

LG278

FREELY ADAPTED FROM THE STORY *"THE PEOPLE OF THE BLACK COAST"* BY ROBERT E. HOWARD
CREATOR OF CONAN

RAID AND BATTLE HAVE THINNED THE PIRATE-SHIP'S CREW-- SCARCELY ENOUGH SPEARMEN REMAIN TO WORK THE LONG GALLEY.

YET, SHE SAILS ON... AND FOR MANY MILES INLAND, WOMEN WHISPER HER NAME TO AFFRIGHT UNRULY CHILDREN--

"BE QUIET, LEST BÊLIT, THE DAUGHTER OF DERKETA COME FOR YOU-- EITHER SHE, OR ELSE HER MATE AMRA, WHO CAN TURN HIMSELF INTO A LION!"

THE SHEMITE SHE-PIRATE MERELY SMILES TO HEAR SUCH TALES.

SHE IS NOT, HOWEVER, SMILING TODAY.

WHY YOUR DARK MOOD, WOMAN?

SHE MAY OR MAY NOT HEAR... BUT SHE CERTAINLY DOES NOT ANSWER.

NEARBY, HOWEVER, A RUMBLE ARISES WHICH WILL NOT BE PUT OFF SO EASILY...

...AND CONAN, KNOWING MORE OF THEIR MUSICAL TONGUE THAN THE BLACK CORSAIRS KNOW, HEARS IT.

YOU'RE ASKING FOR A MUTINY, BÊLIT.

WE'RE SHORT-HANDED, YET YOU WON'T TAKE THE TIME TO RETURN TO THE SOUTHERN ISLES TO RECRUIT MORE MEN... OR AT LEAST GIVE THESE A REST.

I GAVE UP ONE ROYAL TREASURY, MY LOVER-- AND I WON'T REST TILL I'VE WON ANOTHER.

CONAN SCOWLS... FOR HE KNOWS THAT, UNTIL SHE RESTS, NO ONE RESTS.

NOR CAN M'GORA, FIRST AMONG HER SUB-CHIEFS, KEEP THE MEN IN LINE FOREVER.

BACK TO WORK, LAZY ONES!

ARE YOU HYBORIANS, TO FEAR BENDING YOUR BACKS?

AND, WHEN EVEN A RECOVERED N'YAGA SEEKS OUT CONAN, CALLED AMRA...

WE MUST HAVE ONE OR THE OTHER, AMRA... MORE MEN, OR AT THE VERY LEAST A LAYOVER AT SOME PORT!

I KNOW THE SITUATION AS WELL AS YOU, WITCH-MAN.

BUT I ALSO KNOW BÊLIT-- AND HER WILL, IN THAT AREA, MATCHES MY OWN.

STILL, I'LL DO WHAT I CAN....!

DAYS LATER, HOWEVER, THE TIGRESS IS STILL BEARING SOUTHWARD-- FARTHER SOUTH THAN EVER BEFORE-- WHEN THE *DARK CLIFFS* ARE SIGHTED --

--THOSE SELFSAME *DARK CLIFFS* OF LEGEND WHICH, IN YEARS AGONE, HELPED GIVE THE *BLACK COAST* ITS VERY NAME.

SOLID ROCK THEY SEEM TO BE, OF BASALT, HUNDREDS OF FEET HIGH-- AND OTHER, EVEN HIGHER CLIFFS SEEM TO RISE BEYOND THEM, RAMPART ABOVE RAMPART.

WE SHOULD *AVOID* THEM, BÊLIT. THERE'S NO WAY WE COULD CLIMB THEM, EVEN IF WE HEARD THE *TREASURE TROVE OF THE TURANIAN KINGS* WAS NESTLED ON THEIR TOP.

HARSH WORDS FROM A *CIMMERIAN*, MY LOVER. STILL, I AGREE, SO--

WAIT! WHAT'S THAT-- IN THAT ROCKY *INLET?*

WHERE? MY OLD EYES SEE NOTHING--!

NO, SHE'S *RIGHT*, N'YAGA. HO, YOU *LUBBERS!* LOWER A *BOAT!*

THERE'S A *SHIP* MOORED BY THOSE BROODING CLIFFS!

THE BLACK CORSAIRS GRUMBLE SUPERSTITIOUS-LY AMONG THEMSELVES, FOR THE MYTHS SURROUND-ING THE DARK CLIFFS ARE NOT PLEASANT ONES.

YET, THE WORD OF *AMRA* IS SECOND ONLY TO THAT OF *BÊLIT* HERSELF...

THUS, ERE LONG, TWO LONGBOATS DRAW NEAR THE MOORED VESSEL, AS IT TOSSES GENTLY, AIMLESSLY, UPON THE LAPPING WAVES, LIKE A STEER ON A LONG TETHER...

SHE'S *NOT WRECKED*, THEN-- BUT SHE COULDN'T HAVE BEEN HERE *LONG*, ELSE SHE'D SURELY HAVE BEEN DASHED AGAINST THE CLIFF-FACE.

AYE. BUT, IF THERE'S ANYONE ON BOARD, HE MUST BE *HIDING.*

SHE'S *ARGOSSEAN*, BY THE LOOK OF HER, GODDESS.

WELL, THE MERCHANT-MEN OF ARGOS HAVE BEEN KNOWN TO CARRY THEIR FAIR SHARE OF GOLD AND GOODS-- THOUGH I NEVER HEARD OF ONE THIS FAR *SOUTH* BE-FORE.

TRUE, GODDESS. IT WAS ONLY *EXPLORER SHIPS* THAT EVER GOT AS FAR SOUTH AS THE *SILVER ISLES.*

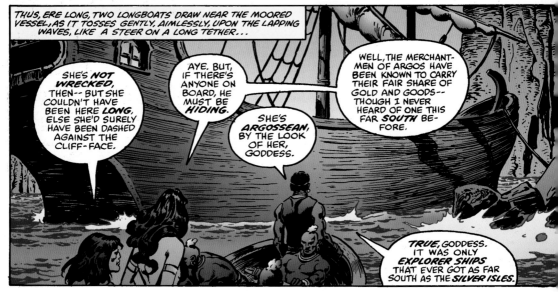

ON BOARD, THE CORSAIRS MAKE A STARTLING DISCOVERY...

GODDESS! AMRA! THIS MAN'S NOT SO LONG DEAD, BUT HIS **HEAD** AND ONE **ARM** HAVE BEEN... **TORN OFF!**

AND **THERE'S** ANOTHER-- OR AT LEAST **HALF** A MAN!

THEY WERE **ARGOSSEANS,** ALL RIGHT. SEARCH THE SHIP!

I LIKE IT LITTLE BETTER THAN THE **MEN,** BÊLIT-- STAYING ON THIS CURSED SHIP WHERE MEN HAVE BEEN TORN LIMB FROM LIMB.

AND **TORN** THEY WERE, NOT SLICED BY SWORDS!

PERHAPS YOU'RE--

GODDESS!

THAT'S **M'GORA!** COME!

WHAT IS IT, M'GORA? **TREASURE?**

I AM **NOT CERTAIN,** GODDESS.

LOOK!

AMOURS OF ISHTAR!

A FEW **GEMS,** AYE...THOUGH THE STONES ARE ONES I'VE NOT SEEN BEFORE...

...AND **GRAVEN GODS** I DARE NOT TOUCH, KNOWING NOT THEIR NAMES OR POWERS!

WHAT DO YOU AND N'YAGA MAKE OF IT, CONAN? YOU'VE BOTH TRAVELED MORE WIDELY THAN I...!

CROM TAKE ME FOR A FOOL, BUT IF I HAD TO GUESS-- I'D SAY THESE WERE CARVED IN **KHITAI.**

KHITAI!? BUT THAT'S ON THE **EASTERN** EDGE OF THE WORLD!

WHAT SAY **YOU,** MY MENTOR?

AMRA KNOWS WHEREOF HE SPEAKS, GODDESS.

IN THE PALACE OF YOUR EARTH- LY FATHER, IN **ASGALUN,** I SAW SUCH IDOLS -- BROUGHT BY **CARAVAN** THROUGH HYRKANIA AND THE INLAND KINGDOMS.

STILL, MEN HAVE EVER SPOKEN OF A **SOUTHERN PASSAGE,** FAR SOUTH OF EVEN OUR **SILVER ISLES.**

PERHAPS THE ARGOSSEANS WERE RETURNING FROM KHITAI BY THAT WAY, WHEN **TRAGEDY** STRUCK.

TRAGEDY? *WHAT* TRAGEDY, WITCH-MAN?

AT THIS POINT, GODDESS, I COULD NOT EVEN GUESS.

WELL, *I* CAN GUESS THAT THIS SHIP CARRIED FAR MORE TREASURE THAN REMAINS ON BOARD. *LOOK!*

MORE CHESTS SAT THERE-- AND *RECENTLY,* TOO, FROM THE ABSENCE OF DUST.

MOMENTS LATER, ABOVE DECKS ONCE MORE...

THERE'S *NOWHERE* THEY COULD HAVE GONE, BUT *INTO* THE CLIFFS THEMSELVES, SINCE THEY'RE TOO STEEP TO CLIMB.

FOR *MEN,* BÊLIT! BUT WE DON'T KNOW WHAT WE'RE UP AGAINST HERE.

WHATEVER TOOK THE CHESTS DOUBTLESS SLEW THE *CREW,* AS WELL.

THE *DEVIL* WITH THE CREW!

WHAT CARE I FOR *DOGS OF ARGOS* SAVE THAT THEY BUILD SHIPS FOR ME TO PLUNDER!?

WE'RE *INVESTIGATING* THAT INLET-- *NOW!*

IF HERE BE THE *TREASURE* I SEEK, IT WILL SAVE US FROM JOURNEYING TO *ANOTHER* PLACE I KNOW OF, BUT FAR HARDER TO REACH!

SOON, THE TWIN LONGBOATS ARE WINDING THEIR TORTUOUS WAY AMONG THE JUTTING ROCKS, OUT OF DIRECT SIGHT OF THE SUN...

WHAT DO YOU *SEE,* MY LOVER?

ONLY A PLACE TO *BEACH* OUR BOATS, IF WE WISH-- FOR WE'VE RUN OUT OF INLET.

THAT'S JUST PRECISELY WHAT WE *SHALL* DO.

I SEE NO SIGNS OF *HUMAN PASSAGE* HERE, THOUGH IT COULD BE THE TIDES HAVE ERASED THEM.

STILL, IF THE ARGOSSEANS CAME HERE AT ALL, IT MUST HAVE BEEN *LATELY* FROM THE LOOK OF THE SHIP...

...AND OF THE *CORPSES* THEREON.

AT THE MENTION OF THE DISMEMBERED BODIES, THE BLACK CORSAIRS STIFFEN...

AND, TRUTH TO TELL, *CONAN* TOO FEELS FAINT CLAWINGS AT THE OUTER EDGE OF HIS BARBARIAN MIND.

LEAVING N'YAGA AND TWO OTHERS BY THE BOATS, THE OTHERS HEAD UPWARD AND INWARD, BENEATH A HEAVY DARK CANOPY OF ROCK THAT IS VIRTUALLY A *CAVE*... OR A *CUL-DE-SAC*.

CAREFUL, M'GORA! THAT'S *SCALDING STEAM* COMING UP FROM THOSE CREVICES-- AND IT SMELLS AS IF *HELL* ITSELF IS NEAR.

THE HYBORIANS CALL IT *SULFUR*, GIRL-- THOUGH IT *IS* WHAT HELL WOULD PROBABLY SMELL LIKE, AT THAT.

THERE MUST BE *PRESSURES* FAR BELOW, WHICH-- *HOLD!*

WHAT *IS* IT?

I DON'T KNOW. SOME KIND OF *CLAW-MARK*... BUT MADE BY SOMETHING THE SIZE OF A LARGE *MAN!*

LET'S GO ON,... BUT MORE *QUIETLY*...!

THEN, AS THE TWO FOREMOST PIRATES STARE ABRUPTLY ACROSS THE *TOP* OF THE ROCKY INCLINE--

ASHTORETH AND ADONIS! WHAT--??

THEY ARE THOSE WHO *MADE* YONDER CLAW-MARKS, WOMAN.

CRABS!

CRABS? YES, PERHAPS-- IF THAT TERM MAY BE STRETCHED TO INCLUDE CREATURES AS *DIFFERENT* FROM A TRUE CRAB AS A MAN IS DIFFERENT FROM ONE OF THE LESSER APES.

TO AND FRO THEY SCUTTLE SILENTLY, SOMETIMES ON TWO LEGS, SOMETIMES ON FOUR... SOME OF THEM CARRYING WHAT APPEAR TO BE *MAN-MADE* ARTIFACTS.

"THE *TREASURE!*" CONAN HEARS BÊLIT BREATHE THE WORD BESIDE HIM.

BUT ALREADY, HIS KEEN EYES ARE UPON SOMETHING *BEYOND* THE DEVIL-CRABS, AS HE THINKS OF THEM...

...SOMETHING PALE AND WAN AND ALL TOO *HUMAN*.

SOMETHING, OR RATHER *SOMEONE* WHO SEES THEM-- BETWEEN BARS CLENCHED BY DESPERATE FINGERS!

WELL, THERE'S YOUR *ARGOSSEAN CREW*, BÊLIT-- PRISONERS OF THOSE *MONSTERS*, WHATEVER THEY ARE.

M'GORA, YOU AND OTHERS FALL BACK TO THE LONG-BOATS, WHILE WE TWO *RECONNOITER*!

YES, AMRA.

ARE YOU STILL FRETTING ABOUT THE *ARGOSSEANS* IN ISHTAR'S NAME?

IT'S THEIR *KHITAN TREASURES* I WANT, NOT--

I MAKE GREAT *ALLOWANCES* FOR YOU, WOMAN, BECAUSE YOU'VE LIVED AS AN *OUTCAST* ALL YOUR LIFE-- EVEN MORE SO THAN I.

BUT I'D NOT LEAVE *ANY* MEN CAPTIVES OF THOSE THINGS, NOT EVEN IF THEY WERE STYGIANS! *COME!*

SINCE THEY'RE *NOT* STYGIANS, I'M COMING!

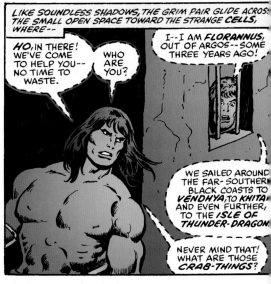

LIKE SOUNDLESS SHADOWS, THE GRIM PAIR GLIDE ACROSS THE SMALL OPEN SPACE TOWARD THE STRANGE *CELLS*, WHERE--

HO, IN THERE! WE'VE COME TO HELP YOU-- NO TIME TO WASTE.

WHO ARE YOU?

I--I AM *FLORANNUS*, OUT OF ARGOS-- SOME THREE YEARS AGO!

WE SAILED AROUND THE FAR-SOUTHERN BLACK COASTS TO *VENDHYA*, TO *KHITA* AND EVEN FURTHER, TO THE *ISLE OF THUNDER-DRAGON*

NEVER MIND THAT! WHAT ARE THOSE *CRAB-THINGS*?

I KNOW NO MORE THAN *YOU*-- SAVE THAT THEY'RE LIKE CRABS, BUT *INTELLIGENT* ONES-- PERHAPS EVEN SMARTER THAN MEN!

WHAT?

WHY DO YOU SAY THAT?

DO YOU SEE THESE ROCK-CARVED *CELLS*, STRANGER?

THE CRAB-MEN *BUILT* THEM-- IN A MATTER OF *HOURS*--

--SIMPLY BY LOOKING AT *DRAWINGS* WE HAPPENED TO HAVE ON BOARD!

HOW MANY *OTHERS* ARE WITH YOU?

SOME OF MY CREW STILL LIVE-- BUT NOT FOR *LONG*, MAY MITRA HELP US!

WHAT DO YOU **MEAN**, MAN?

IT'S...NOT EASY TO RELATE... EVEN NOW.

"THEY MUST HAVE **SENT** THOSE THOUGHTS TO ME...BECAUSE THEY WANTED HUMAN BEINGS AS **SPECIMENS** OF SOME SORT.

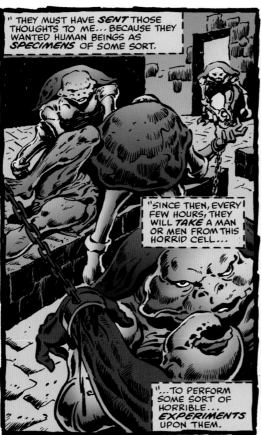

"SINCE THEN, EVERY FEW HOURS, THEY WILL **TAKE** A MAN OR MEN FROM THIS HORRID CELL...

"...TO PERFORM SOME SORT OF HORRIBLE... **EXPERIMENTS** UPON THEM.

"THEY TOOK OUR **TREASURE**, TOO -- JEWELS AND CARVED STATUARY WE RISKED OUR LIVES TO TRADE FOR.

"TO THEM, THE GEMS ARE OF **NO VALUE**, I KNOW, SAVE TO THEIR HELLISH CURIOSITY.

"I DON'T KNOW **HOW** I SENSE THIS, FOR THEY DO NOT SPEAK... BUT I CAN **FEEL** THEIR THOUGHTS, SOMEHOW."

VE MOORED OUR SHIP BUT A DAY OR SO AGO...SOME **WHIM** OF MINE...ONLY TO BE **CAPTURED** BY THE CRAB-MEN.

MITRA HELP ME, I HAD HOPED TO SHOW THE KING OF ARGOS THAT HE NEED NOT SEND CARAVANS **OVERLAND** TO TRADE WITH KHITAI AND VENDHYA ..

BUT NOW, MY DREAM IS TURNED INTO **NIGHT-MARE!** CAN YOU--?

GODS! THEY'RE HERE! I CAN SAY NO MORE.

BACK, YOU FIENDS FROM THE PIT! HAVEN'T YOU TORTURED US **ENOUGH**?

BUT THE UNSPEAKING CRUSTACEANS PAY NO MORE HEED TO FLORANNUS'S OUTCRY THAN WE TO THE UP-TURNED HEAD OF AN ANT...

...AS THEY DRAG FORTH YET AN-OTHER SCREAMING, WRITHING, UNFORTUNATE FROM THE MAKESHIFT DUNGEON.

FLORANNUS! HELP ME, CURSE YOU! **HELP MEEE!!**

NO! IN MITRA'S NAME -- **SPARE ME!**

HEEDLESS OF HIS OWN SAFETY, THE ARGOSSEAN EXPLORER RUSHES FORWARD-- ONLY TO FIND HIS OWN *PIKES* BARRING HIS WAY.

YOU FILTHY, INHUMAN *MURDERERS!*

OR PERHAPS HE WISHES MERELY TO *SHIELD* THOSE AT THE WINDOW BEHIND HIM.

WELL, WOMAN? YOU *SAW.*

IF YOU INSIST, I'LL GO IT *ALONE,* BUT I'LL NOT LEAVE THOSE MEN TO--

NO, YOU WERE *RIGHT,* CONAN.

WE'LL SAVE THEM. *AND* THEIR TREASUR

MOMENTS LATER, WHEN THE CRAB-THINGS HAVE DEPARTED AGAIN...

FLORANNUS! MY NAME IS CONAN, AND MY CAPTAIN *BÊLIT* AND I INTEND TO RESCUE YOU, IF WE CAN.

WHAT FEW THERE ARE *LEFT* OF US TO RESCUE-- BUT I THANK YOU.

THEN TAKE OFF YOUR *LEATHER SHIRTS*--AND HURRY!

YOU HEARD THE MAN, YOU SEA-DOGS! *OFF* WITH THEM!

BUT, CAPTAIN-- DID YOU HEAR THE NAME *BÊLIT?* A *PIRATE--!*

WHAT MATTERS *THAT?* THOSE TWO ARE OUR ONLY CHANCE.

AND KEEP YOUR VOICE *DOWN,* FOR THE GODS' SAKE!

WITHIN MINUTES...

GOOD! WHATEVER THEIR SINISTER INTELLIGENCE OR THOUGHT POWERS, THE DEVIL-CRABS HAVEN'T SORTED *OUR* THOUGHTS OUT YET FROM *YOURS.*

THAT WINDOW'S *TOO SMALL* FOR YOU TO ESCAPE, EVEN IF I RIP OUT THE BARS, SO I NEED SOME ADDITIONAL *WEIGHT...*

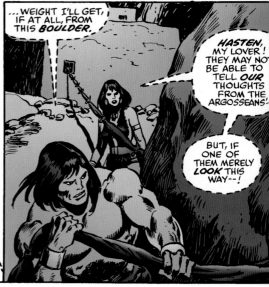

...WEIGHT I'LL GET, IF AT ALL, FROM THIS *BOULDER.*

HASTEN, MY LOVER! THEY MAY NO* BE ABLE TO TELL *OUR* THOUGHTS FROM THE ARGOSSEANS!

BUT, IF ONE OF THEM MERELY *LOOK* THIS WAY--!

THEY'VE NOT DONE SO *YET*, AND ANOTHER FEW SECONDS MAY BE *TOO LATE*-- I HOPE!

NOW, WITH ALL THE SINEWY STRENGTH STORED IN HIS GARGANTUAN FRAME, CONAN ARCHES HIS MIGHTY *BACK* AGAINST THE MASSIVE BOULDER...

...POISED *PRECARIOUSLY* AS IT IS ATOP A ROCKY *LEDGE*.

AS THE HUGE ROCK SLOWLY BEGINS TO TILT BENEATH THE CIMMERIAN'S FIERCE ONSLAUGHT, THE *BARS*, IMBEDDED DEEP INTO THE CRAB-FASHIONED *CLAY*, BEGIN TO EXERT A TREMENDOUS PRESSURE UPON BOTH...

IT'S *WORKING*, CONAN! JUST A BIT MORE--!

I'M-- DOING ALL I *CAN!*

IF ONLY THE *LEATHER* HOLDS-- A FEW SECONDS LONGER THAN THAT POORLY MADE *CLAY*--!

IT DOES.

THE *BARS* HOLD FIRM-- BUT THE *CLAY* ITSELF GIVES WAY--

--AND THE SAILORS OF ARGOS LOOK OUT MORE CLEARLY INTO THE TWILIGHT GLOOMINESS OF THE CAVERN.

HE *DID* IT-- TOPPLED THAT BOULDER OVER THE EDGE!

OF COURSE! DON'T STAND THERE *GAPING*, ARGOSSEAN!

THAT SOUND MAY WELL BRING THE *DEVIL-CRABS* ON THE RUN.

BUT WE'RE *NOT* LEAVING HERE WITHOUT YOUR *EASTERN TREASURE*. WHERE IS IT?

THIS WAY! I'LL BE GLAD TO DIVIDE IT WITH YOU, IN EXCHANGE FOR--

WE'LL DISCUSS THAT LATER.

RIGHT NOW, JUST LEAD THE WAY!

THERE IT IS! I SAW THE CRAB-MEN CARRY IT IN HERE.

BY BEL, GOD OF ALL THIEVES!

THIS IS MADNESS, WOMAN! BURDENED DOWN THIS WAY, WE'LL NEVER--

CONAN-- BEHIND YOU!

WHAT THE DEVIL--?

A DEVIL-CRAB!

EVEN AS IT ENTERS THE LOW DOOR- WAY, THE GREAT CRUSTACEAN RAISES ITS PINCERLIKE CLAWS--

--SO THAT IT CATCHES FAST THE BARBARIAN'S FURIOUSLY DOWN- THRUST BLADE!

CROM! IT'S AS IF THE THING READ MY MIND--

--LIKE THAT SEA- WITCH DID! *

* LAST ISSUE.--R.T.

CONAN DARES NOT RELINQUISH HIS SWORD OR WAIT FOR AID-- EVEN AS THE HUGE MANDIBLES SNAP GREEDILY FOR HIS FACE...

YET, HIS OWN MENTION OF THE SEA-WOMAN HAS SET HIS MIND RACING.

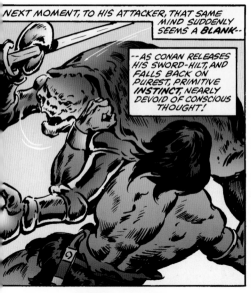

NEXT MOMENT, TO HIS ATTACKER, THAT SAME MIND SUDDENLY SEEMS A *BLANK*--

--AS CONAN RELEASES HIS SWORD-HILT, AND FALLS BACK ON PUREST, PRIMITIVE *INSTINCT*, NEARLY DEVOID OF CONSCIOUS THOUGHT!

AND BY THE TIME THE MONSTER CAN AGAIN *DISCERN* THE CIMMERIAN'S MENTAL PATTERNS--

--IT MAKES NO DIFFERENCE AT ALL.

MOTHER OF MITRA!

YET, EVERY *HUMAN BRAIN* THERE ABRUPTLY FEELS A NEEDLE-SHARP *THOUGHT* PIERCE IT-- AS IF THE CRAB-THING IS CALLING FOR *HELP!*

IT'S STILL *ALIVE*-- BUT IT CAN'T HARM US WITHOUT ARMS.

GRAB THE *LOOT*-- AND LET'S GET THE HELL OUT OF HERE!

I HOPE YOU REALIZE WHAT YOU'VE LET US *IN* FOR, BÊLIT.

WE'RE SLOWED TO A *CRAWL* WITH ALL THIS JUNK--

--AND HERE COME THE *DEVIL-CRABS* HOT ON OUR TRAIL!

ONWARD THEY COME-- THEIR CRUEL *THOUGHT EMANATIONS* STRIKING THE FLEEING HUMANS ALMOST LIKE A PHYSICAL THING...

KEEP MOVING, DOGS!

THEY'LL TAKE THOSE CHESTS DOWN TO *HELL* WITH THEM, IF THEY DON'T LET GO OF--

HOLD! WE'RE ON A LITTLE *INCLINE* HERE...

...AND THIS REMINDS ME OF A *GAME* I'VE SEEN THE HYBORIANS PLAY, IN THE COURTYARDS OF NEMEDIA.

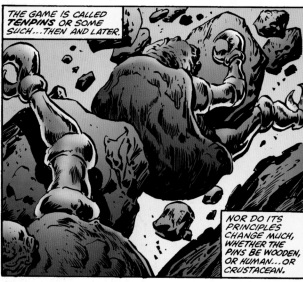

THE GAME IS CALLED *TENPINS* OR SOME SUCH...THEN AND LATER.

NOR DO ITS PRINCIPLES CHANGE MUCH, WHETHER THE PINS BE WOODEN, OR HUMAN...OR CRUSTACEAN.

WELL, THAT'S WON US A *RESPITE*... BUT THAT'S ABOUT ALL.

AYE! WE'RE FLEEING THE *WRONG WAY* DAMN THEIR HIDES--*INTO* THIS CUL-DE-SAC, INSTEAD OF DOWN TOWARD--

CONAN! THAT BOULDER DOWN THERE-- *LOOK!*

WOMAN, I THINK YOU'VE JUST *MADE UP* UP FOR ALL YOUR WILFULLNESS.

FLORANNUS--SEE THOSE *SEVERAL BOULDERS* DOWN THERE, WITH *STEAM* GUSHING UP WHERE THEY'RE SET IN THE GROUND?

YOU AND YOUR MEN PUSH SOME ROCKS FROM UP HERE, AIMED AT *DISLODGING* THEM IF YOU CAN!

YES--I SEE YOUR *PLAN.*

BUT, THE CRAB-MEN WILL BE UPON US, BEFORE WE CAN--

CONAN'S ANSWER RAISES THE FLESH ON THE ARGOSSEAN'S SCALP.

WITHOUT A WORD OR BACKWARD GLANCE, HE *LEAPS OFF* THE INCLINE, BROADSWORD IN HAND AND BARBARIAN WAR-CRY ON HIS LIPS --

--AND INTO THE VERY **MIDST** OF THE ONCOMING **DEVIL-CRABS!**

A MOMENT LATER, CONAN IS UP AND **RUNNING** ONCE MORE--

--ONLY HIS NEED FOR **RASH ACTION** KEEPING HIM FROM MENTALLY BETRAYING HIS PLAN--

--SO THAT THE **SHELL-THINGS** PURSUE HIM, THINKING THE OTHERS HOPELESSLY TRAPPED IN THE **CUL-DE-SAC** ABOVE.

ABOVE, HOWEVER, THE SEAMEN HAVE FOUND STILL ANOTHER OF THE MANY FREE-LYING **BOULDERS** WHICH ABOUND ON THE INCLINE...

SHOULDERS TO IT, MEN!

...SO THAT, EVEN AS THE CIMMERIAN HAS NEARLY RUN OUT OF ROOM TO FLEE TO....!

THAR SHE BLOWS!

BE IT MITRA, CROM, OR AN IMPERSONAL FATE-- **SOMEONE** IS KIND THIS DAY TO PIRATES AND SAILORS ALIKE --

--AS ONE GREAT BOULDER STRIKES THE OTHER, FROM BENEATH WHICH POWERFUL, SULFUROUS **BURSTS OF STEAM** ARE EMITTED.

NEXT INSTANT, ELEMENTAL FORCES HELD IN CHECK PERHAPS FOR **UNTOLD EONS** ARE SUDDENLY AND IRREVERSIBLY UNLEASHED--

--EVEN AS THEIR OWN FORWARD **MOMENTUM** CARRIES THE DEVIL-CRABS INTO THE MIDDLE OF THE FIRE-HOT **HOLOCAUST!**

FOR THOSE FIRST FEW MOMENTS, THE CREATURES' **NATURAL ARMOR**-- WHICH COULD RESIST A SWORD WIELDED BY ANY MAN WEAKER THAN CONAN OF CIMMERIA-- IS ABRUPTLY RENDERED **USELESS**, AS STEAM CREEPS INTO EVERY CREVICE...

...TO **ROAST** THE CRAB-THINGS ALIVE!

THE **LAST** THOSE ATOP THE INCLINE SEE OF THEIR DELIVERER, HE IS RACING MADLY **AHEAD** OF THE CASCADING STEAM.

THEN THEY COVER HIM... AND HE IS SEEN NO MORE.

HE'S **ALIVE**, THANK THE GODS-- IF ONLY HE REMAINS SO!

AYE... AND THE STEAM **COOLS** JUST ENOUGH, BY THE TIME IT REACHES US, THAT IT ONLY MAKES US **SWEAT**, NOT PERISH.

BUT, WHAT WILL HAPPEN WHEN THE INITIAL BURST OF STEAM **DIES DOWN?**

FOR LONG MINUTES, THE SEA-FARERS HUDDLE IN SUCH SHELTER AS THEY CAN FIND...

THEN, WHEN NATURE'S PENT-UP ANGER IS LARGELY *SPENT*, SO THAT THE STEAM WHICH POURS FORTH FROM SUBTERRANEAN CAVERNS IS NO GREATER THAN THAT FROM THE OTHER GUSHERS SEEN EARLIER...

MITRA! ALL THE MONSTERS ARE *DEAD*, IT SEEMS.

THEY WERE SUPERIOR TO MEN, IN MANY WAYS-- YET *INFERIOR* TO US, IN WAYS WE COULD NEVER HAVE SUSPECTED.

BUT WHERE IS *CONAN*? IF HE'S BEEN *KILLED*--!

NOT JUST *YET*, MY LOVE...

I FOUND SHELTER OF MY *OWN*, AS YOU CAN SEE.

ANYONE FOR *STEAMED CRAB-MEAT*?

JUST THEN, *M'GORA* RETURNS WITH SEVERAL BLACK CORSAIRS, SPEARS AT THE READY...

THIS IS THE *END* OF OUR ALLIANCE, ARGOSSEANS. WE'LL SPARE YOU...BUT THE *TREASURE* IS OURS.

BÊLIT, FOR CROM'S SAKE--!

WE'VE NO CHOICE, IT SEEMS. BUT I PRAY YOU, LEAVE US *SOME* OF IT, IN ALL FAIRNESS--

--TO PAY MY MEN, AND TO CONVINCE THE *HYBORIANS* IT WOULD PAY THEM TO SAIL THE SOUTHERN PASSAGE TO THE *DISTANT EAST!*

WELLLLL...YOUR MEN *DID* PUSH DOWN THE BOULDER THAT SAVED US ALL, FLORANNUS.

ALL RIGHT! WE'LL *SPLIT* THE LOOT EQUALLY, AND YOU CAN BE ON YOUR WAY.

SOME TIME AFTERWARD, THE ARGOSSEAN GALLEY SAILS OFF NORTHWARD, BOUND FOR MESSANTIA...

GETTING *GENEROUS* IN YOUR OLD AGE, ARE YOU, WOMAN?

DON'T PLAY THE *FOOL*, MY LOVER! YOU KNOW FULL WELL WHY I LET THEM TAKE SOME OF THE PLUNDER BACK HOME.

IF SHIPS OUT OF ARGOS AND ZINGARA BEGIN TO PLY THESE SEAS ON THEIR WAY EAST, THERE'LL BE *MORE SHIPPING* FOR ME TO LOOT THAN EVER BEFORE!

IT WAS *WISDOM* MADE ME ACT THUS, NOT WOMANLY WEAKNESS.

THAT'S MY *BÊLIT*-- ASHAMED EVEN TO ADMIT YOU MIGHT HAVE AN UNSELFISH IMPULSE NOW AND--

WHAT THE DEVIL--?

N'YAGA! HE'S REELING! HELP ME!

IT'S...NOTHING! JUST... FELT *FAINT* FOR A MOMENT...

MUST HAVE BEEN... SOME AFTER-EFFECT OF ONE OF THE *SCRATCHES* I GOT, LEAPING LIKE A FROG AMID THE ROCKS.

PERHAPS... THOUGH NONE OF YOUR SCRATCHES SO MUCH AS DREW BLOOD.

NO MATTER. THE WEAKNESS IS *PASSING* ALREADY.

STILL, I WOULD *EXAMINE* YOU MORE CLOSELY, AMRA. I COULD--

NO, SHAMAN... LET IT BE.

SHALL WE PUT TO *SEA* NOW, BÊLIT?

NOT... JUST *YET*, BELOVED.

OH? AND WHY *NOT*?

SURELY MY REMARKS ABOUT *CRAB-MEAT* DIDN'T--

HARDLY! BUT THERE'S STILL SOME *PLUNDER* LEFT IN THE CAVES BACK THERE.

AND AS LONG AS THE CRAB-MEN SEEM ALL *DEAD*, WE MIGHT AS WELL...

HAH! YOU'RE A *PIRATE* THROUGH AND THROUGH, AREN'T YOU, WOMAN?

AND WHAT ELSE *SHOULD* I BE, PRAY TELL?

LOWER ANOTHER *LONGBOAT*, THEN--

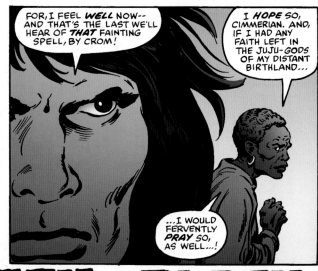

FOR, I FEEL *WELL* NOW-- AND THAT'S THE LAST WE'LL HEAR OF *THAT* FAINTING SPELL, BY CROM!

I *HOPE* SO, CIMMERIAN. AND, IF I HAD ANY FAITH LEFT IN THE JUJU-*GODS* OF MY DISTANT BIRTHLAND...

...I WOULD FERVENTLY *PRAY* SO, AS WELL...!

NEXT. ISSUE: **AT LAST!** THE MIGHTIEST CONAN EPIC OF ALL! **DEATH** ON THE **BLACK COAST!**

HER SHEMITISH EYES NARROWING, BÊLIT LOOKS AT THE VERDANT, VINE-TANGLED SCENE BEFORE THEM...

THIS IS THE *RIVER ZARKHEBA*, WHICH IS *DEATH*, CIMMERIAN.

ITS WATERS ARE *POISONOUS*, IT'S SAID-- SEE HOW *DARK* AND *MURKY* THEY RUN?

ONLY *VENOMOUS REPTILES* LIVE IN THAT RIVER-- THE BLACK PEOPLE *SHUN* IT.

SO YOU TOLD ME *ONCE BEFORE*, WHEN WE PASSED ITS MOUTH. *

YOU SAID THEN THERE WAS A *STORY* YOU'D TELL ME SOMETIME...

AYE, SO I DID... AND SURELY, THE *TIME* IS COME FOR YOU TO HEAR IT--

*ISSUE #60. --ROY.

"NOT LONG BEFORE *YOU* JOINED ME, I WAS PURSUING A HATED *STYGIAN GALLEY* DOWN THE KUSHITE COAST.

REACHING THE MOUTH OF THE ZARKHEBA, IT *FLED* UP THE RIVER...

"I ANCHORED' IN THIS VERY SPOT, AND *WAITED*...

"FOR, THE JUNGLE WAS SO *FORBIDDING*, I WAS CERTAIN IT WOULD SOON BE FORCED TO *TURN BACK*.

"DAYS LATER, THE GALLEY *DID* COME FLOATING DOWN THE DARK WATERS...

"BUT, ITS DECKS WERE *BLOOD-STAINED*...AND *DESERTED*!

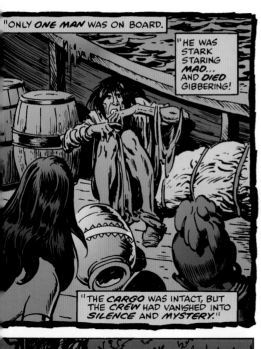

"ONLY *ONE MAN* WAS ON BOARD.

"HE WAS STARK STARING *MAD*... AND *DIED* GIBBERING!"

"THE *CARGO* WAS INTACT, BUT THE *CREW* HAD VANISHED INTO *SILENCE* AND *MYSTERY*."

MY LOVER, I BELIEVE THERE IS A *CITY* SOMEWHERE ON THAT RIVER-- FOR, I'VE HEARD TALES OF *GIANT TOWERS* AND *WALLS* GLIMPSED FROM AFAR.

WE FEAR NOTHING, YOU AND I! LET US GO AND *SACK* THAT CITY!

CONAN'S NOD IS ALL THE AGREEMENT THE SHE-PIRATE NEEDS.

IT MATTERS LITTLE TO *HIM* WHERE THEY SAIL... OR WHOM THEY FIGHT.

THUS, WITH ITS BATTLE-THINNED CREW, THE *TIGRESS* ROUNDS THE MYSTERIOUS *BEND* WHICH SHUTS OUT SIGHT OF THE SEA...

...AND *SUNSET* FINDS THEM FORGING STEADILY AGAINST THE SLUGGISH FLOW...

..AVOIDING *SANDBARS* WHERE STRANGE REPTILES COIL.

ONCE, AN *INHUMAN VOICE* IS LIFTED IN AWFUL *MOCKERY* FROM SOMEWHERE, FAR OFF...

THE CRY OF AN *APE*, BÊLIT SAYS.

CONAN...DO YOU *FEAR* THE GODS?

I WOULD NOT *TREAD* ON THEIR *SHADOW.*

WHAT **OF** YOUR **GODS**? I'VE NEVER HEARD YOU CALL ON THEM FOR **AID**-- ONLY **SWEAR** BY THEM.

THEIR CHIEF IS **CROM**-- HE DWELLS ON A GREAT MOUNTAIN.

WHAT **USE** TO CALL ON HIM? LITTLE **HE** CARES IF MEN LIVE OR DIE!

BETTER TO BE **SILENT** THAN TO CALL HIS ATTENTION TO YOU-- HE WILL SEND YOU **DOOMS**, NOT FORTUNE.

HE IS GRIM AND LOVELESS, BUT AT **BIRTH** HE BREATHES POWER TO **STRIVE** AND **SLAY** INTO A MAN'S SOUL.

WHAT **ELSE** SHALL MEN ASK OF TH' GODS?

AND WHAT OF **LIFE AFTER DEATH**, MY LOVER?

I KNOW **NOT**, NOR DO I **CARE**. I KNOW ONLY **THIS**--

LET ME **LIVE DEEP** WHILE I LIVE, WHILE **PHILOSOPHERS** BROOD.

I **LIVE**... I BURN WITH LIFE... I LOVE, I SLAY, AND AM **CONTENT**.

YET, THE GODS ARE **REAL**... AND THERE **IS** LIFE AFTER DEATH, I KNOW.

I KNOW **THIS**, TOO, CONAN OF CIMMERIA...

MY LOVE IS STRONGER THAN ANY **DEATH**!

MY **HEART** AND **SOUL** ARE WELDED TO **YOURS**.

WERE I STILL IN **DEATH**, AND YOU FIGHTING FOR YOUR **LIFE**-- I WOULD **COME BACK** FROM THE ABYSS TO **AID** YOU!

I AM **YOURS**, CONAN-- **YOURS**--

--AND ALL THE **GODS** AND ALL THEIR **ETERNITIES** SHALL NOT **SEVER** US!

AAA...

WHAT THE **DEVIL**--

THE **LOOKOUT**!

IN AJUJO'S NAME-- **HELP!!**

I'M COMING, LABOTO!

CONAN'S GREAT SWORD *HEWS* THROUGH THE TRUNK OF THE GIGANTIC SERPENT--

--AND *BLOOD* DRENCHES THE RAILS AS THE DYING MONSTER SWAYS *FAR OUT!*

THEN, STILL GRIPPING ITS VICTIM, IT *FALLS*-- TO SINK INTO THE *RIVER*, COIL BY COIL--

--LASHING THE WATER TO BLOODY FOAM--

--IN WHICH *MAN* AND *REPTILE* VANISH TOGETHER.

HE'S... *GONE.*

DO NOT BLAME *YOURSELF*, AMRA.*

THERE WAS *NOTHING* YOU COULD HAVE DONE TO *SAVE* HIM.

*AMRA IS THE NAME BY WHICH CONAN IS KNOWN ALONG THE BLACK COAST. --ROY.

BUT NOW, I WILL SAY WHAT I *HELD BACK* FROM SAYING BEFORE--

TURN BACK, BÊLIT! THERE IS *UNKNOWN, POWERFUL EVIL* IN THIS HELLISH PLACE!

YOU SAY THAT, N'YAGA? YOU, WHO LIVED FOR YEARS AMONG *CIVILIZED* MEN?!

VERY *WELL* THEN, MY MENTOR. *I'LL* NOT TURN BACK...

...YET, I'LL HAVE *NO MAN* WITH ME WHO DOES NOT COME *WILLINGLY.*

WE *RESPECT* OUR AGED SHAMAN, GODDESS... BUT WE STAND BY *YOU.*

THEN... *SO SHALL* I.

M'GORA, YOU OTHERS-- WHAT *SAY* YOU?

THE MATTER, THEN, IS *SETTLED.*

WE GO ON!

CONAN HOLDS HIS PEACE, BUT THEREAFTER KEEPS THE LOOKOUT WATCH *HIMSELF.*

HOWEVER, NO *OTHER* HORROR COMES CRAWLING UP FROM THE MURKY DEPTHS THIS NIGHT...

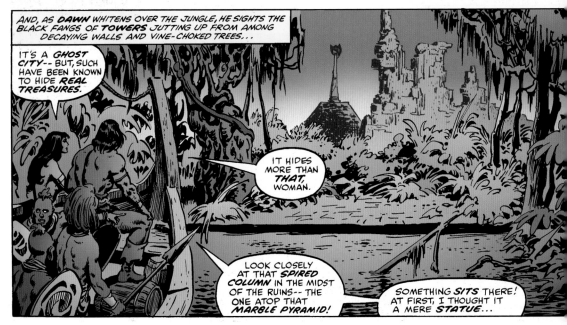

AND, AS *DAWN* WHITENS OVER THE JUNGLE, HE SIGHTS THE BLACK FANGS OF *TOWERS* JUTTING UP FROM AMONG DECAYING WALLS AND VINE-CHOKED TREES...

IT'S A *GHOST CITY*-- BUT, SUCH HAVE BEEN KNOWN TO HIDE *REAL TREASURES.*

IT HIDES MORE THAN *THAT*, WOMAN.

LOOK CLOSELY AT THAT *SPIRED COLUMN* IN THE MIDST OF THE RUINS-- THE ONE ATOP THAT *MARBLE PYRAMID!*

SOMETHING *SITS* THERE! AT FIRST, I THOUGHT IT A MERE *STATUE...*

...BUT THEN, I SAW IT *MOVE.* IT'S *ALIVE!*

"IT'S A *GREAT BIRD,"* SAYS ONE OF THE WARRIORS, STANDING IN THE BOWS.

"IT'S A MONSTER *BAT,"* INSISTS ANOTHER.

"IT'S AN *APE,"* SAYS BÊLIT, MATTER-OF-FACTLY.

JUST THEN, THE CREATURE SPREADS *BROAD WINGS...*

...AND *FLAPS OFF* INTO THE JUNGLE.

A *WINGED APE!*

BETTER WE HAD *CUT OUR THROATS* THAN COME HERE! IT IS *HAUNTED!*

FOR ONCE, YOU *DISAPPOINT* ME, N'YAGA.

HELMSMAN! GUIDE HER *IN!*

SOON, THE PIRATE GALLEY IS TIED TO THE CRUMBLING *WHARF...*

AND, WITHIN MOMENTS, THE CORSAIRS MAKE A *PICTURESQUE SIGHT* AMONG THE RUINS, OVER WHICH BROODS A *SILENCE* AS SINISTER AS THAT OF A SLEEPING SERPENT.

THAT MUST HAVE BEEN THE *TEMPLE OF THE OLD ONES.*

LOOK! YOU CAN SEE THE *CHANNELS FOR BLOOD* ALONG THE SIDES OF THE ALTAR...

...AND EVEN THE RAINS OF *10,000 YEARS* HAVE NOT WASHED THE *DARK STAINS* FROM THEM!

YOU'VE A GOOD EYE FOR *BLOOD,* I'LL SAY *THAT.*

BUT-- WHO WERE THESE "OLD ONES" YOU SPEAK OF?

I KNOW *NOT!* NOT EVEN IN *LEGENDRY* IS THIS CITY MENTIONED...

BUT LOOK AT THE *HANDHOLDS* AT EITHER END OF THE ALTAR!

PRIESTS OFTEN CONCEAL THEIR *TREASURES* BENEATH SUCH SACRED STONES.

FOUR OF YOU-- *LAY HOLD* AND SEE IF YOU CAN *LIFT* IT!

I'LL NEED THREE OF YOU TO *HELP* ME.

WE CAN *MANAGE* IT, ALL THE SAME.

NOW, WHEN I SAY *HEAVE...*

GODDESS! AMRA! THE HANDHOLDS ARE SOMEHOW-- *NOT* CUT OUT FOR *HUMAN* HANDS.

NO-- *WAIT!*

NOW WHAT?

I HEARD A *SERPENT* HISS IN THE GRASS, MY LOVER.

COME HERE, AND *SLAY* IT!

I HEARD *NOTHING*... BUT, *ALL RIGHT!*

THE *REST* OF YOU-- BEND YOUR *BACKS* TO THE STONE!

I DON'T SEE A *THING,* WOMAN. ARE YOU *SURE* YOU--?

HEAVE, CORSAIRS--

HEAVE!

BY *AJUJO!* THE *ALTAR*-- IT IS *TURNING* SUDDENLY--

--TURNING ON ITS *SIDE!* WHAT--?

AS THE GREAT STONE *REVOLVES,* THERE IS SIMULTANEOUSLY A *GRINDING RUMBLE* ABOVE--

--AND, BEFORE THEY CAN ESCAPE, THE *LOOMING TOWER* COMES CRASHING DOWN UPON *FOUR WARRIORS*--

--BURYING THEM BENEATH *BROKEN MASONRY!*

YOU-- *KNEW* OF THIS, GIRL?

I MERELY *SUSPECTED*... SO I EMPLOYED A *RUSE* TO LURE *YOU* AWAY.

AND LET *YOUR OWN* MEN BE KILLED?!

THE *OLD ONES* GUARDED THEIR TREASURE *WELL*...AND I WOULD NOT CHANCE *LOSING* YOU!

CONAN SAYS *NO MORE,* FOR NO WORDS OF HIS WOULD BRING *DEAD MEN* BACK TO LIFE.

BUT, AS THE STONES ARE CLEARED AWAY, HE SENSES THAT A *SUBTLE CHANGE* HAS COME OVER HIS *MATE* SINCE SIGHT- ING THE *LOST CITY.*

NEVER BEFORE WAS SHE SO *UNCARING* OF THE CORSAIRS WHO SERVE HER SO FAITHFULLY.

THEN, AS THE *LAST STONE* IS ROLLED AWAY...

ISHTAR! THERE-- IN THE *CRYPT* BENEATH WHERE THE *ALTAR* STOOD--!

DIAMONDS-- EMERALDS-- SAPPHIRES-- GEMS I'VE NEVER *SEEN* BEFORE, NOT EVEN AS A CHILD IN THE *PALACE AT ASGALUN!*

I'LL BUY MY *OWN* COUNTRY WITH THESE!

AND *THIS* IS THE BEST TREASURE OF *ALL!*

CONAN NOTES ONLY THAT THE LONG STRING OF *CRIMSON STONES* BÊLIT HAS PULLED FROM THE TROVE--

--LOOK TO HIM LIKE CLOTS OF *FROZEN BLOOD,* STRUNG ON A THICK GOLD WIRE.

GODDESS! AMRA! *BEHOLD!*

THE *DEVIL-APE*-- RISING FROM THE DECKS OF THE *TIGRESS!*

NEVER *MIND* THAT! MAKE A *LITTER* TO BEAR THESE *JEWELS* BACK TO--

TO LOOK AT THE *GALLEY!*

WHERE THE DEVIL ARE *YOU* GOING??

THAT *THING* MAY HAVE KNOCKED A *HOLE* IN THE BOTTOM, FOR ALL WE KNOW!

DAMN!

WELL?

THAT FLYING DEMON HAS **STAVED** IN OUR WATER CASKS!

WE WERE **FOOLS** NOT TO HAVE LEFT A MAN ON GUARD-- WE **CAN'T** DRINK THIS **RIVER** WATER.

I'LL TAKE **M'GORA** AND SOME MEN, AND SEARCH THE JUNGLE FOR **FRESH** WATER.

BÊLIT STARES BACK AT HIM **VAGUELY**, IN HER EYES THE BLANK BLAZE OF HER **STRANGE PASSION**... HER FINGERS WORKING AT THE **CRIMSON GEMS** ON HER BREAST...

VERY WELL. I'LL GET THE **LOOT** ABOARD.

THE **LIGHT** AROUND THEM CHANGES SWIFTLY FROM GOLD TO **GRAY**, AS CONAN AND THE WARRIORS HEAD OFF IN **SINGLE FILE** THROUGH THE ARCHING GREEN BRANCHES...

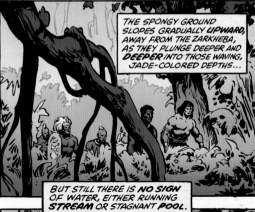

THE SPONGY GROUND SLOPES GRADUALLY **UPWARD**, AWAY FROM THE **ZARKHEBA**, AS THEY PLUNGE DEEPER AND **DEEPER** INTO THOSE WAVING, JADE-COLORED DEPTHS...

BUT STILL THERE IS **NO SIGN** OF WATER, EITHER RUNNING **STREAM** OR STAGNANT **POOL**.

HALT, M'GORA!

WHAT **IS** IT, AMRA?

I'M... NOT SURE.

THOUGHT I HEARD SOMETHING... AS IF WE'RE BEING FOLLOWED.

YOU AND THE OTHERS MARCH STRAIGHT ON TILL YOU CAN NO LONGER SEE ME-- THEN STOP AND WAIT FOR ME.

YES, AMRA... BUT TAKE CARE!

CONAN WATCHES WITH *ADMIRATION* AS THE *STALWART BLACK CORSAIRS* GO FORWARD OUT OF *LOYALTY* TO HIM, SUPERSTITIOUS THOUGH THEY ARE...

YET, WHEN THEY'VE VANISHED FROM SIGHT, HE HEARS *NOTHING ELSE.*

SUDDENLY, HOWEVER, HE REALIZES THAT THE VERY *AIR* AROUND HIM IS IMPREGNATED WITH AN *ALIEN* AND *EXOTIC SCENT.*

SOMETHING GENTLY BRUSHES HIS *TEMPLE...*

...AS A CLUSTER OF CURIOUSLY LEAFED *STALKS* WITH GREAT DARK *BLOSSOMS* NODS AT HIM...!

THE BLACK LOTUS!

HE *RECOGNIZES* THAT FLOWER WHOSE JUICE IS *DEATH* --

--AND WHOSE *SCENT* BRINGS DREAM-HAUNTED *SLUMBER.*

BUT ALREADY, HE FEELS A SUBTLE, IRRESISTIBLE *LETHARGY* STEALING OVER HIM.

EVEN *HE* CAN BARELY HEAR THE *RATTLE* THAT EMERGES FROM HIS THROAT.

M'GORA...!

INSTANTLY, THE JUNGLE ABOUT HIM *DIMS* BEFORE HIS EYES...

...NOR DOES HE HEAR THE *TERRIBLE SCREAMS* WHICH BURST OUT, NOT FAR AWAY... AS HIS *KNEES* COLLAPSE, AND HE PITCHES LIMPLY TO THE EARTH!

AND, ABOVE HIS PROSTRATE FORM, THE *GREAT BLACK BLOSSOMS* NOD IN THE *WINDLESS AIR.*

IN CONAN'S **MIND,** HOWEVER, THE WINDS BLOW-- CLOUDS DISPERSE-- AND A **HUGE CITY** RISES ON THE BANKS OF A WIDE **RIVER,** FLOWING THROUGH AN ILLIMITABLE **PLAIN.**

THROUGH THIS CITY MOVE **ALIEN FIGURES...** CAST IN HUMANITY'S MOLD, YET DISTINCTLY **NOT** MEN...

WINGED AND OF HEROIC PROPORTIONS, THEY RESEMBLE **MAN** ONLY AS MAN IN HIS HIGHEST FORM RESEMBLES THE **GREAT APES.**

AND, WHEN THEY REAR THEIR COLOSSAL CITY, MAN'S PRIMAL **ANCESTORS** HAVE NOT YET RISEN FROM THE SLIME OF THE **PRIMORDIAL SEAS.**

THESE BEINGS ARE **MORTAL,** THOUGH THE INDIVIDUAL SPAN OF LIFE IS **ENORMOUS.**

THEN, THE GREAT RIVER AND ITS SHORE-REGION **ALTER--**

PLAINS TURN INTO **SWAMPS** THAT STINK WITH **REPTILIAN LIFE...**

WHERE FERTILE MEADOWS ONCE ROLLED, **FORESTS** REAR UP, GROWING INTO DANK **JUNGLES...**

TERRIFIC **CONVULSIONS** SHAKE THE EARTH, AND THE NIGHTS ARE LURID WITH SPOUTING **VOLCANOES** THAT FRINGE THE DARK HORIZONS WITH **RED PILLARS...**

AN **EARTHQUAKE** SHAKES THE HIGHEST TOWERS OF THE CITY...

...CAUSING THE **RIVER** TO RUN **JET-BLACK** FOR DAYS WITH SOME **LETHAL SUBSTANCE** SPEWED UP FROM THE SUB-TERRANEAN DEPTHS.

MANY **DIE** WHO DRINK OF IT...

AND, IN THOSE WHO **SURVIVE**, THE DRINKING BRINGS **CHANGE**... SUBTLE, GRADUAL, AND GRISLY.

THEY WHO HAVE BEEN **WINGED GODS** BE-COME PINIONED **DEMONS**...

...WITH ALL THAT REMAINS OF THEIR ANCESTORS' VAST KNOWLEDGE **DISTORTED** INTO GHASTLY PATHS!

THEIR RACE **DIES FAST** NOW-- BY CANNIBALISM, AND BY HORRIBLE **BLOOD-FEUDS** FOUGHT OUT IN THE MURK OF THE MID-NIGHT JUNGLE.

AT LAST, AMONG THE LICHEN-GROWN **RUINS** OF THEIR CITY, ONLY A **SINGLE SHAPE** LURKS...

...A STUNTED, ABHORRENT PERVERSION OF NATURE.

NOW, FOR THE FIRST TIME, **HUMANS** APPEAR... FIFTY WARRIORS OUT OF **PREHISTORIC STYGIA**.

DEFEATED BY A STRONGER TRIBE, THEY HAVE **FLED**-- TO LOSE THEM-SELVES IN THE GREEN OCEAN OF JUNGLE AND RIVER.

EXHAUSTED, THEY LIE DOWN AMONG RUINS WHERE **RED BLOSSOMS** BLOOM ONCE IN A CENTURY, TO WAVE BENEATH A **FULL MOON**.

AND, AS THEY SLEEP, A **HIDEOUS FORM** CREEPS FROM THE SHADOWS...

..TO PERFORM *WEIRD* AND *AWFUL RITES* ABOUT AND ABOVE *EACH SLEEPER.*

AROUND THE STYGIANS, CRIMSON BLOSSOMS GLIMMER LIKE *SPLASHES OF BLOOD.*

THEN, THE MOON GOES *DOWN...* AND THE EYES OF THE *NECROMANCER* ARE RED JEWELS SET IN THE EBONY OF NIGHT.

WHEN *DAWN* SPREADS ITS BRIGHT VEIL OVER THE RIVER, THERE ARE *NO MEN* TO BE SEEN...

...ONLY A *HAIRY WINGED HORROR* THAT SQUATS IN THE CENTER OF A RING OF FIFTY GREAT SPOTTED *HYENAS...*

...BEASTS THAT POINT QUIVERING MUZZLES TO THE GHASTLY *SKY* AND HOWL LIKE *SOULS IN HELL.*

NOW, SCENE FOLLOWS SCENE *SWIFTLY:*

BLACK MEN COME UP THE RIVER, IN SKULL-PROWED BOATS...

...TO *FLEE,* OR ELSE *DIE SCREAMING* AS VAMPIRE EYES BLAZE REDLY.

THERE ARE *GRISLY FEASTS* BENEATH THE MOON, ACROSS WHOSE *SCARLET DISC* A *BATLIKE SHADOW* INCESSANTLY SWEEPS.

THEN, ABRUPTLY, AND ETCHED MORE **CLEARLY,** AROUND THE JUNGLED POINT IN THE WHITENING DAWN SWEEPS A **LONG GALLEY.**

IT IS AT **THIS** POINT THAT CONAN FIRST REALIZES HE IS **DREAMING...**

...THOUGH HE STILL DOES **NOT** AWAKEN.

IT IS THRONGED WITH **SHINING, EBON FIGURES...**

AND, IN THE **BOWS** STANDS A GRIM, BRONZE-SKINNED **GIANT,** BROADSWORD IN HAND.

IN A JUNGLE GLADE, HE SEES **M'GORA** AND MORE THAN A SCORE OF **BLACK SPEARMEN,** STANDING AS IF **WAITING** FOR SOMEONE.

NOW, EVEN AS HE REALIZES IT IS FOR **HIM** THEY WAIT, HE HEARS THEIR SUDDEN **YELLS OF FEAR...**

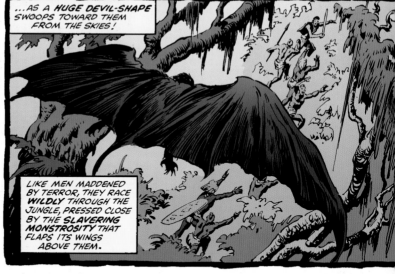

...AS A **HUGE DEVIL-SHAPE** SWOOPS TOWARD THEM FROM THE SKIES!

LIKE MEN MADDENED BY TERROR, THEY RACE **WILDLY** THROUGH THE JUNGLE, PRESSED CLOSE BY THE **SLAVERING MONSTROSITY** THAT FLAPS ITS WINGS ABOVE THEM.

AND THEN, WITH A SAVAGE EFFORT-- CONAN **BREAKS** THE UNSEEN CHAINS WHICH HOLD HIM TO HIS DREAMS...

NEAR HIM, SWAYING GENTLY, IS THE DUSKY *LOTUS*...

...AND HE HASTENS TO *DRAW AWAY* FROM IT.

THEN, IN THE *SPONGY SOIL* NEARBY, HE SEES A TRACK-- AS IF SOME *ANIMAL* HAD PUT A TENTATIVE FOOT FORWARD...

...ONLY TO WITH-DRAW IT AGAIN.

IT LOOKS LIKE THE SPOOR OF AN UNBELIEV-ABLY LARGE *HYENA.*

NEXT, AS THE *FADING LIGHT* TELLS HIM THE DAY NEARS ITS *END*...

M'GORA!

THE JUNGLE *SILENCE* MOCKS HIM.

A *PANIC* RISES IN HIM, AS HE FOLLOWS HIS *CORSAIRS'* TRACKS...

...ONLY TO BEHOLD SUDDENLY THE VERY *GLADE* HE'D BEHELD IN HIS *LOTUS-DRUGGED* DREAM...

...AND, IN IT, THE *SHIELDS* AND *SPEARS* OF THE *BLACK PIRATES!*

FROM THEIR TRACKS, CONAN KNOWS THE SPEARMEN *FLED* WILDLY.

HE SEES THAT HE DRAWS NEAR A HILL-LIKE *ROCK* WHICH SLOPES STEEPLY...

...WHEN, *SUDDENLY,* HE HEARS A *SOUND* BEHIND HIM--

WHO THE DEVIL--?

FOR AN INSTANT, HE THINKS IT A GREAT, DARK-FURRED **GORILLA** OUT OF HIS FLOWERY **NIGHTMARE.**

THEN, HIS EYES SQUINTING, THEN GROWING WIDE-- HE KNOWS THE **TRUTH**--

YOU--?

M'GORA?!

THE **CREATURE** BEFORE HIM **CROUCHES** APELIKE, LONG ARMS DANGLING, **FROTH** DRIPPING FROM LOOSE LIPS.

HIS FACE IS AN **INHUMAN MASK**--

--AS, WITH A SOBBING **ANIMAL-CRY,** THE STRONG-MUSCLED BLACK **CHARGES**--!

M'GORA-- **KEEP BACK!** I DON'T WANT TO--

GRARRR

YET, HIS **TEETH** GLEAMING LIKE **FANGS,** HIS **EYES** ROLLING, THE **CORSAIR BITES** AND **CLAWS** AT HIM--

--UNTIL--

UHNNNH--!!

HIS SKIN CRAWLING WITH THE **HORROR** WHICH MADNESS ALWAYS INSTILLS IN THE SANE, CONAN LOOKS DOWN AT THE MAN HE HAS JUST **STABBED.**

M'GORA HAS BEEN ALLY... COMRADE-IN-ARMS...**FRIEND.**

NOW, THE CIMMERIAN HAS HIS **BLOOD** BOTH ON HIS **SWORD**...

...AND ON HIS **HANDS.**

WITH A SHUDDER, CONAN STRIDES TO THE **CLIFF'S EDGE** NEARBY...ALREADY **HALF AWARE** OF WHAT HE WILL **SEE** FROM THERE.

ON THE JAGGED ROCKS BELOW LIE **M'GORA'S SPEARMEN,** IN LIMP, DISTORTED ATTITUDES THAT TELL OF CRUSHED LIMBS AND SPLINTERED BONES.

NOT ONE MOVES.

AND THERE ARE THOSE **CLOSE BY** WHO KNOW THAT THEY **NEVER SHALL.**

FOR A LITTLE SPACE, CONAN STANDS **MOTIONLESS...**

THEN, WITHOUT WARNING, HE **WHEELS**-- RUNNING BACK THE WAY HE'S **COME**--

-- FLINGING HIMSELF WITH **RECKLESS HASTE** THROUGH THE TALL GRASS AND BUSHES--

-- **HURDLING** CREEPERS THAT SPRAWL SNAKELIKE IN HIS PATH.

HIS **SWORD** SWINGS LOW IN HIS RIGHT HAND--

-- AND AN UNACCUSTOMED **PALLOR** TINGES HIS FACE AT THE **SUNSET'S** FINAL GLEAMING.

THEN, AMID THE DIM TWILIGHT OF THE **RIVER SHORE**, HE LOOKS ONCE MORE ON **DEATH** AND **DESTRUCTION...**

CROM!

AND ALL **ABOUT** THE BODIES, AND PIECES OF BODIES, ARE SWARMS OF **HUGE FOOTPRINTS...** LIKE THOSE OF **HYENAS.**

NEXT, CONAN COMES SILENTLY UPON THE PIER...

...ABOVE WHOSE DECK IS SUSPENDED SOMETHING THAT GLIMMERS IVORY WHITE IN THE GATHERING DARKNESS...

AND, SPEECHLESS, HE LOOKS UPON THE QUEEN OF THE BLACK COAST--

--AS SHE HANGS FROM THE YARD-ARM OF HER OWN GALLEY!

BETWEEN THE YARD AND HER THROAT STRETCH A LINE OF CRIMSON CLOTS THAT SHINE LIKE BLOOD IN THE GRAY LIGHT.

LATER--

THE MOON HAS NOT YET RISEN AS CONAN SITS LIKE AN IRON STATUE ON THE PYRAMID AMONG THE FALLEN TOWERS.

THE OTHER DEAD LIE AS THEY HAVE FALLEN.

BUT, ON THE DECKS OF THE TIGRESS, ON A PYRE OF BROKEN BENCHES, SPEAR SHAFTS, AND LEOPARD-SKINS, LIES BÊLIT IN HER LAST SLEEP, WRAPPED IN HIS OWN SCARLET CLOAK.

LIKE A TRUE QUEEN SHE LIES, WITH HER SEA-PLUNDER HEAPED HIGH ABOUT HER...

...BUT NOT THE CURSED RICHES OF ZARKHEBA, WHICH LIE BENEATH THE SULLEN WATER.

NO LONGER, AS THE MOON RISES, DOES HE **DOUBT** THE VISIONS OF THE **BLACK LOTUS**.

WHY **HE** HAS BEEN SPARED SO LONG, HE DOES NOT **UNDERSTAND**... UNLESS THE **MALIGN ENTITY** WHICH RULES THE RIVER MEANS TO **TORTURE** HIM WITH GRIEF AND FEAR.

NOW, SOMETHING **MOVES** IN THE BLACKNESS UNDER THE TREES BELOW.

CONAN HAS **LONG SINCE** SENSED THAT HIS UNKNOWN ENEMY WILL **CONCLUDE** THE DRAMA BY SENDING HIM AFTER THE **OTHER** VICTIMS OF HIS **MAD MAGIC**.

AND NOW, FROM THE SHADOWS, TWENTY GREAT **SPOTTED HYENAS** COME SILENTLY, SWIFTLY, RUNNING LOW.

TWENTY, ONLY! SO, CONAN MUSES, THE PIRATES **SPEARS** TOOK THEIR TOLL, AFTER ALL.

THE HYENAS' SLAV-ING **FANGS** FLAS IN THE MOONLIGH THEIR **EYES** BLAZI AS NO **TRUE BEAS** EYES EVER BLAZED

THEN, TEETH GRITTED, CONAN DRAWS **NOCK** TO EAR...

AND, AT THE **TWANG** OF THE STRIKE, A **FLAME-EYED SHADOW** BOUNDS HIGH -- TO **FALL**, WRITHING!

THE **REST** DO NOT FALTER.

ONWARD THEY COME...

--DRIVEN WITH ALL THE **FORCE** AND **ACCURACY** OF STEELY THEWS--

AND, LIKE A **RAIN OF DEATH,** AMONG THEM FALL THE **ARROWS** OF THE **CIMMERIAN**--

YYIII

--BACKED BY A **HATE** HOT AS THE SLAG-HEAPS OF **HELL!**

AMID THIS FEATHERED DESTRUCTION, LESS THAN **HALF** THE HUGE WERE-BEASTS REACH EVEN THE **FOOT** OF THE PYRAMID.

BY WHAT **GODLESS ALCHEMY** THESE BEINGS HAVE BEEN BROUGHT INTO EXISTENCE, THE BERSERK BARBARIAN **CANNOT GUESS**...

BUT HE KNOWS HE FACES **DIABOLISM** HERE, BLACKER THAN THE **WELL OF SKELOS!**

HIS **LAST** ARROW GONE NOW, HE DRAWS HIS **SWORD**--

--AND THE **FIRST** OF THE CREATURES TO REACH HIM IS **SHORN ASUNDER!**

BACK, YOU DEVILS THAT ONCE WERE MEN!

HIS MAIL-SHIRT HAS PROTECTED HIS FLESH FROM THAT RARE WERE-BEAST WHO GETS THROUGH HIS METALLIC ARC OF DEATH--TILL NOW--!

CROM'S DEVILS!

YOU'RE THE *LAST* OF THEM, HAIRY ONE--

SO *GO*, AND VENT YOUR HYENA-HOWLS IN THE *WORLD BEYOND!*

ARRRGHH

YET, THE MAIMED BEAST'S CRY IS HIDEOUSLY *MANLIKE* AS IT 'S HURLED WITH BONE-SPLINTERING FORCE AGAINST A JUTTING *COLUMN*--

--LEAVING ITS HUMAN FOE *REELING* ON WIDE-BRACED LEGS, AND GASPING FOR BREATH.

STOOPING, HE STARTS TO GROPE FOR HIS *SWORD* AMONG THE LIFELESS FORMS THAT SPRAWL AT HIS FEET--

--WHEN *SUDDENLY*, FROM A DISTANCE ABOVE, HE HEARS THE SOUND OF *FLAPPING WINGS*--

--AND TURNS TO SEE A *GREAT SHADOWY SHAPE* OUTLINED HORRIBLY AGAINST THE *MOON!*

YET, EVEN AS HE READIES HIMSELF INSTANTLY FOR AN ATTACK FROM THE *AIR*--

--THE *PYRAMID* STAGGERS ABRUPTLY AND AWFULLY *BENEATH* HIM!

STARTLED, HE HEARS A *RUMBLING CRACKLE*--

--AND BEHOLDS THE *TALL COLUMN* ABOVE HIM, WAVING LIKE A *WAND!*

STUNG TO GALVANIZED *LIFE,* HE BOUNDS FAR OUT--

HIS FEET HIT A *STEP* HALFWAY DOWN THE STAIRS, WHICH *ROCK* UNDER HIM--

--AND HIS *NEXT* DESPERATE LEAP CARRIES HIM *CLEAR!*

EVEN THEN, WITH A SHATTERING CRASH LIKE A BREAKING MOUNTAIN-- THE PYRAMID CRUMPLES!

FOR A BLIND, CATACLYSMIC INSTANT, THE VERY SKY SEEMS TO RAIN SHARDS OF MARBLE.

THEN, A RUBBLE OF SHATTERED STONE LIES WHITELY UNDER THE MOON.

CONAN STIRS, RECOVERING FROM THE GLANCING BLOW THAT COST HIM HIS HELMET...

UNNNH--!!

YET, ACROSS HIS LEGS, WHICH MAY OR MAY NOT BE BROKEN--

--LIES A GREAT PIECE OF THE COLUMN, PINNING HIM DOWN.

AT THAT MOMENT, SOMETHING SWEEPS DOWN ACROSS THE STARS TO STRIKE THE SWORD NEAR HIM...

THE WINGED ONE!

WITH A FEARFUL SPEED IT IS RUSHING UPON HIM--

AND, THOUGH CONAN LITERALLY THROWS HIS ACHING BODY TOWARD HIS FALLEN SWORD--

--HIS CLAWING FINGERS MISS IT-- BY INCHES!

DESPERATELY NOW, HE STRAINS UPWARD AGAINST THE SHARD WHICH PINS HIS LEGS-- AND, AS HIS VEINS SWELL IN HIS TEMPLES, IT GIVES SLOWLY!

YET, LONG BEFORE HE CAN FREE HIMSELF, HE KNOWS THE MONSTER WILL BE UPON HIM WITH ITS GREAT, BLACK-TALONED HANDS--

FOR, THE HEAD-LONG RUSH OF THE WINGED ONE HAS NOT WAVERED--

AND NOW, IT TOWERS OVER THE PROSTRATE CIMMERIAN LIKE A DARK SHADOW OF DEATH!

THEN-- A GLIMMER OF WHITE FLASHES BETWEEN THAT SHADOW AND ITS VICTIM!

IN ONE MAD INSTANT, SHE IS THERE--

--A TENSE PALE SHAPE, VIBRANT WITH LOVE AS FIERCE AS A SHE-PANTHER'S--

--AND SHE CRIES OUT-- A SHARP AND RINGING CRY--

GNNRRK

--AS SHARP AS THE RING OF **STEEL** AS SHE THRUSTS AT THE **APISH** CREATURE'S **BREAST!**

BÊLIT!!

AND THEN, HE REMEMBERS THE **WORDS** OF HIS **MATE** --

--THE WORDS SHE SPOKE SO PASSIONATELY ON THE **DECKS** OF THE **TIGRESS** --

"WERE I STILL IN **DEATH,** AND YOU FIGHTING FOR YOUR **LIFE,** I WOULD **COME BACK** FROM THE ABYSS TO **AID** YOU!!!"

THEN, SHE IS **GONE** -- AND HE SEES ONLY THE **WINGED FIEND,** STAGGERING BACK IN UNWONTED **FEAR** --

--ARMS **LIFTED** AS THOUGH TO FEND OFF **ATTACK!**

WITH ONE TERRIBLE, VIOLENT EFFORT, HE **HEAVES UPWARD** A FINAL TIME--

--HURLING THE STONE ASIDE!

BY NOW, THE *WINGED ONE* IS COMING ON AGAIN--

--AND *CONAN* SPRINGS TO *MEET* IT, HIS VEINS ON FIRE WITH *MADNESS!*

THE *THEWS* STAND OUT LIKE *CORDS* ON HIS FOREARMS AS HE SWINGS HIS GREAT *SWORD*--

--AND HIS *SWEEPING ARC* SHEARS CLEAR THROUGH THE MONSTER'S *HAIRY FORM!*

AAAAA

FOR A LONG MOMENT, THOSE *RED EYES* GLARE UP AT HIM WITH *AWFUL LIFE*--

--AS THE BARBARIAN STANDS IN THE *MOONLIT SILENCE,* THE DRIPPING SWORD SAGGING IN HIS HAND, LOOKING DOWN AT THE SEVERED REMNANTS OF HIS *ENEMY.*

THEN, THOSE *TALONED HANDS* *KNOT* SPAS-MODICALLY-- *STIFFEN*--

--AND THE **OLDEST RACE** IN THE WORLD IS **EXTINCT.**

AS FOR THE **BEAST-THINGS** WHICH HAD BEEN THE MONSTER'S SLAVES AND EXECUTIONERS...THEY HAVE REVERTED TO **MEN** NOW...

...HAWK-FACED, DUSKY-SKINNED MEN, TRANSFIXED BY **ARROWS** OR MANGLED BY **SWORDSTROKES...**

...AND CRUMBLING TO **DUST** BEFORE HIS EYES.

TURNING ON HIS HEEL, THE CIMMERIAN STRIDES DOWN THE ROTTING WHARFS TO THE **GALLEY.**

A FEW SLASHES OF HIS BLADE CUTS HER **ADRIFT.**

ROCKING SLOWLY IN THE SULLEN WATER, THE TIGRESS SLIDES OUT SLUGGISHLY TOWARD THE **MIDDLE** OF THE RIVER...

...AS CONAN, ON THE SWEEP, FIXES HIS GAZE ON THE **CLOAK-WRAPPED SHAPE** THAT LIES IN STATE ON THE **PYRE...**

...A **PYRE** THE **RICHNESS** OF WHICH IS EQUAL TO THE RANSOM OF AN **EMPRESS.**

THEN, THE **CURRENT** CATCHES THE SHIP, AND CARRIES HER DOWN TOWARD THE WAITING **SEA.**

Later--

ONCE MORE, **DAWN** TINGES THE OCEAN, AS A **REDDER GLOW** LIGHTS ITS MOUTH.

CONAN OF CIMMERIA LEANS ON HIS GREAT SWORD UPON THE WHITE BEACH, WATCHING THE **TIGRESS** SWINGING OUT ON HER **LAST VOYAGE.**

NO **HAND** IS AT HER SWEEP, NO **OARS** DRIVE HER THROUGH THE GREEN WATERS.

BUT, A CLEAN, TANGING **WIND** BELLIES HER SILKEN SAIL...

AND, AS A WILD SWAN CLEAVES THE SKY, SHE SPEEDS **SEAWARD**, FLAMES MOUNTING **HIGHER AND HIGHER** FROM HER DECK TO LICK AT THE MAST...

...AND ENVELOP THE **PALE, STILL FIGURE** THAT LIES LAPPED IN SCARLET ON THE SHINING PYRE.

TO CONAN, BÊLIT **WAS** THE SEA-- SHE LENT IT **SPLENDOR** AND **ALLURE**.

WITHOUT HER, IT ROLLS A BARREN, DREARY, AND DESOLATE **WASTE** FROM POLE TO POLE.

SHE **BELONGS** TO THE SEA... AND TO ITS EVERLASTING MYSTERY HE HAS **RETURNED** HER.

HE CAN DO NO MORE.

FOR HIMSELF, ITS GLITTERING BLUE EXPANSE IS NOW MORE **REPELLANT** THAN EVEN THE LEAFY FRONDS WHICH RUSTLE AND WHISPER **BEHIND** HIM, TELLING OF VAST, MYSTERIOUS **WILDS** BEYOND... A GRIM FOREST INTO WHICH HE NOW MUST **PLUNGE**.

AND SO **PASSES** THE QUEEN OF THE BLACK COAST...

...AS, LEANING ON HIS RED-STAINED SWORD, CONAN STANDS **SILENTLY** UNTIL THE RED GLOW HAS **FADED**, FAR OUT IN THE BLUE HAZES...

...AND **DAWN** SPLASHES ITS ROSE AND GOLD OVER THE TRACKLESS OCEAN.

FIN

EXT-- A NEW CHAPTER BEGINS!
SUE

The Death of Bêlit

A Few Personal Notes on
Conan the Barbarian #91–100
by Roy Thomas

These comics stories written and drawn in the 1978–79 period point to the tragic conclusion of the "Queen of the Black Coast" storyline that had begun two years earlier, in **Conan the Barbarian #58** . . . in some ways, in #57. Ever since then, I'd known I wished to conclude it in issue #100 by adapting the grand finale of Robert E. Howard's story of that title. In other words—the death of Bêlit, the she-pirate.

But I still had a few other matters to attend to, before I got to that dramatic denouement.

In issue #91's "Savage Doings in Shem!" I launched the return of the curvaceous corsair and her Cimmerian paramour to Asgalun, the city we'd established as the site of her royal father's death. Lots of setup to do, leaving little room for the kind of magical menace I tried to toss into every issue of **Conan**, since the genre is called "sword-and-sorcery." The oversize swamp rats didn't *quite* provide that element. Neither did Zula's hypnosis of one of the black corsairs. But the Stygian Ptor-Nubis does have the ability to merely touch someone and make him/her obey his commands, and that's gotta count for something.

For penciller John Buscema, no doubt the high point of the issue was drawing Bêlit's seductive dance . . . fairly steamy stuff for a late-seventies Code-approved comic book. But then, Big John always said he didn't care that much for drawing sword-wielding women warriors like Bêlit, Valeria, and Red Sonja; he preferred drawing dancing girls. Luckily for us all, he drew both species equally well.

I felt constrained, on the letters page, to explain why the issue was heavier on plot and lighter on sorcerous action than usual. Up till now, Marvel had not contracted the rights to adapt or utilize the portion of the Conan canon written by Robert E. Howard's "posthumous collaborator" L. Sprague de Camp . . . including non-Conan stories by REH which de Camp had rewritten and edited into tales of the Cimmerian. Now we had that right—but it meant that suddenly the Asgalun of the Howard/de Camp story "Hawks over Shem" was considerably different in cast and history from what we had postulated in **CtB**. Hence the lengthy flashback, intended to bring the two versions of Shem's capital in line. I apologized for that fact that "Savage Doings in Shem!" was perhaps "a bit top-heavy on cloak-and-dagger intrigue and political bedfellows in Asgalun" . . . and pledged to get back to straight-ahead action ASAP.

The next issue was basically a fill-in pencilled by John's talented brother Sal. The note on that tale's splash page said it was done while John "was enjoying a brief but well-earned vacation in France and Italy." That statement may well be true—for John did like to make periodic trips to Italy, his ancestral homeland. Be that as it may, in #92 Sal and I adapted "The Thing in the Crypt," a de Camp/Carter tale of Conan's youth . . . but because of this volume's prescribed page count, it couldn't be reprinted here. Maybe some other time and place.

With #93 we completed the Asgalun episode, and made Bêlit—if very, very briefly—a queen in fact as well as in fantasy. We'd been working toward this end for some time . . . but frankly, I was quite happy to see it come and go.

With #94's "The Beast King of Abombi!," John and I plunged into one of my favorite storylines of the Conan/Bêlit era, for a four-issue serial of sorts.

At the beginning of the issue, we wrote out Zula by having him leave the *Tigress*, accompanied by a few of the black corsairs. This was necessary for two reasons. First, since the doom of everyone on the pirate ship was only half a year away, we had to get rid of Zula if we didn't want to have to kill him off—and I most definitely did not. He was and remains my favorite among the handful of characters I co-created for the Conan color comic (not counting Red Sonja, who's a special case). Second, it had been well established by REH in **The Hour of the Dragon** (AKA **Conan the Conqueror**) that, some years in the future, a deposed King Conan of Aquilonia would again run into several of the black corsairs who'd sailed with him . . . and he couldn't very well do that if they stayed with the vessel and got themselves butchered, could he? So Zula and a few others had to go.

The main storyline owed a debt to Howard's prose tale "Beyond the Black River," which took place years after **CtB** #94. In it, Conan, by then a frontier scout for Aquilonia fighting in the Pictish wilderness, recalls a "curious symbol" he had seen twice in his younger years—the second time, scratched by "a black witch-finder of Kush . . . in the sand of a nameless river." It was a symbol sacred to an ancient god of men and beasts called Jhebbal Sag.

Well, if I was ever going to tell the tale behind that reference, this was the time—for Conan was now a pirate along the Black Coast, and northerners tended to refer to all of the black lands as "Kush," though that was actually just the name of one particular kingdom. Writing and drawing a monthly comic about Conan necessarily meant filling in many gaps between the events in his life recorded by Robert E. Howard, but I preferred, when I could, to fill them with something that grew out of the Texas author's own work.

But "Beyond the Black River" was not the only REH source of inspiration for this story arc. Looking just now at the name of the "Beast King of Abombi"—*Ajaga*—I was reminded instantly that that name, like Jhebbal Sag, came from Howard. In "The Scarlet Citadel," a chained King Conan faces a gigantic black tormentor who plans to wreak a private vengeance on him. "I know you from of old," says his enemy. "Do you remember the sack of Abombi, when your seawolves swarmed in? Before the palace of King Ajaga you slew a chief and a chief fled from you. It was my brother who died; it was I who fled. I demand of you a blood-price, Amra!" (Amra, of course, was the name—meaning "Lion"—by which Conan was known when he sailed with Bêlit.) This "sack of Abombi" almost *had* to occur during Conan's "Black Coast period"—so I made that Ajaga a king of both beasts and men, in this four-part saga.

In our comics version, it is N'yaga, the old shaman who sails on the *Tigress*, who first tells Conan about Jhebbal Sag. (Oh, and one little private joke I sneaked into this issue: I have Ajaga call two of his sub-chiefs "Krato" and "Beeya." If that seemed familiar to some Marvel readers, it might've been because "Kratos" and "Bia" were two minor Greek deities created by the dramatic Aeschylus for his great tragedy **Prometheus Bound**. The words mean "force" and "might" in Greek, and I had used more authentic forms of the characters earlier in a couple of issues of **The Avengers**.

In issue #95, as the plot rolled along, I had the Cimmerian battle a man-size, newly discovered type of dinosaur I'd been reading about. A decade-plus later, audiences watching Stephen Spielberg's film **Jurassic Park** would come to know them as "velociraptors." Old G'Chambi, introduced and killed off in this issue, became the "black witch-finder of Kush" who first shows Conan the sign of Jhebbal Sag. Sometimes it surprised me that it was so easy, so natural, to tie up loose ends in the Conan saga—that things just seemed to "fall into place." Part of the reason, of course, is that, for all of its minor lapses and inconsistencies, the world REH created for his barbarian hero is a well-realized one, needing only a few details here and there to make it come to life in the four-color medium, as well!

This storyline, continuing through #96, also gave me a chance to bring back the great black lion Sholo, whom Conan had inherited when he had killed the original Amra (of the comic book, anyway)—a red-haired evil Tarzan type you can read about in **Volume 9** of this series.

CtB #97 gave me another opportunity for a little private joke—though it concerns the mag's cover, which is not reprinted herein. The scene I asked John Buscema to draw there, of Bêlit leaping over and past Conan, who's chained to a stone altar for sacrifice, at Ajaga, who's raising his ceremonial knife, is an homage to Frank Frazetta's masterwork painting that had been used, a few years earlier, as the cover of the Lancer paperback **Conan the Avenger.**

The one sad note was one I found almost inevitable. I felt that, dramatically, the black lion Sholo should perish fighting for his new master's life. I felt a genuine sadness when I wrote those panels, even though Sholo was never more than lines drawn by pencil and ink on a piece of paper.

"Sea-Woman," in #98, marked a new beginning of sorts. I may (or may not) have already had it in mind to use Howard's poem of that name as the springboard of a story. But I do recall that a young woman named Danette Couto and I were standing in line waiting to see a movie somewhere in L.A. when I mentioned I had to get a new plot out to Buscema the next day. However it happened, Danette (who later changed her first name legally to Dann, and her last to Thomas—by marrying me) came up with the notion of the *Tigress* encountering a sea-tossed female who was both more and less than human, and who lured a few corsairs to watery graves before she was dispatched. Her turning to seaweed at the end harked back to a 1954

Sub-Mariner story written and drawn by my old friend Bill Everett . . . who had doubtless borrowed it from somewhere else. Later, Glenn Lord, the ever-helpful literary agent for the REH estate, gave me permission to quote all of Howard's copyrighted poem "Sea-Woman," which I'd read in a book of REH's poetry. The result, I think, was a moderately haunting vignette.

"Devil-Crabs of the Dark Cliffs," in #99, was perhaps a bit less successful. I needed one more standalone story before #100 . . . and I was aware Howard had written a modern-day story called "The People of the Black Coast," in which stranded seafarers encounter giant, intelligent, humanoid crabs. The "Black Coast" of that tale had no connection with the one in the Hyborian Age, but the name just begged for me to shoehorn it into the Conan saga.

Perhaps I should have resisted that siren call, just as Conan had eventually resisted the song of the Sea-Woman. It was a reasonably good story, but it's easier to write about "giant, intelligent, humanoid crabs" than it is to *show* them without their looking a bit farcical. John Buscema could draw damn near anything and make it look good, but somehow the Devil-Crabs (deviled crabs?) eluded him . . . or else maybe he thought the whole notion so ridiculous he didn't really try that hard. I do know that, in retrospect, when I look at the first panel in which they appear, I'm reminded less of the kind of Lovecraftian horror REH clearly meant to impart, than of the Teenage Mutant Ninja Turtles who'd come along a few years down the line.

Well, they can't all be winners, right? And I did enjoy the beginning and end of the story. In moody captions on the splash page, I was able to work in a few phrases quoted from "Queen of the Black Coast"—and on the final page, I was as amused as Conan at the thought that Bêlit wasn't about to let a little thing like dead Devil-Crabs strewn about stop her from going back to their caves and gathering the plunder she'd left there.

The next issue, however, was one I had both been looking forward to and dreading for some time. A year earlier, science-fiction writer Harlan Ellison had phoned me and volunteered to write the 100th issue of **Conan the Barbarian**, which he knew was coming up. I was flattered, and would've loved to have had Harlan plot a **CtB** issue sometime . . . but not #100. That one was spoken for, well in advance . . . and I intended to do it all myself. (Well, with a little help from John Buscema and inker Ernie Chan, of course!)

Actually, the story was already plotted out for me—far more than any other issue since #58. I won't rehash it here, since you've probably already read its thirty-three pages. I believe that, at an early stage, I'd planned to adapt this fearful finale over the course of #99-100. Somewhere along the line, though, I had convinced publisher Stan Lee to make #100 an extra-sized issue, costing fifty percent more than a regular one and having more than fifty percent more story.

The only problems were ones I'd known were coming. For one thing, in Howard's prose story, Bêlit behaves in a treacherous way toward some of her crew, allowing them to be killed by falling masonry which she had suspected of being booby-trapped by the ancients. In the original story, Conan doesn't remark unfavorably on her behavior. But the Bêlit of the comic books was a character the readers had lived with for three years—and someone the hero loved. So I felt I had to give Bêlit just the slightest excuse for her abominable behavior, as if she were almost bewitched by these old ruins . . . while Conan accepts her actions largely because he realizes that "a subtle change has come over his mate since sighting the lost city."

The rest of the story unfolds pretty much as Howard had envisioned, although M'Gora (N'Gora in REH) had long since become a major and sympathetic character in the comics before he goes mad in this issue and Conan has no choice but to kill him. In REH, he's merely a "sub-chief" who seems to mean nothing in particular to the barbarian. The scene actually has more force, I think, when the Cimmerian must slay his trusted friend . . . then look down at his still form with regret, as if M'Gora's blood is "both on his sword . . . and on his hands."

As to the climactic scene in which the ghostly apparition of the deceased Bêlit shows up to gain Conan the few precious seconds he needs to get free and renew his battle against the winged man-ape . . . well, since REH describes her as "a tense white shape," with a "lithe figure, shimmering like ivory beneath the moon" as "her bosom heaved," her ghostly presence should actually be nude in this sequence.

But you can't have everything.

Somehow, though, I feel as if I personally had just about everything—having a chance to write **Conan the Barbarian** for a decade. I would script fifteen more issues of **CtB** in a row after #115, covering the Cimmerian's journey north through the black kingdoms . . . even adapting a bit of prose from an incomplete Conan story at one point . . . before quitting the book with #115. By then, having reached an impasse with Marvel's management, I'd signed a contract with DC Comics to begin working there as soon as my present contract ran out . . . and while I could have scripted several more issues of **CtB** before I left, I preferred to quit with #115, which was the comic's tenth-anniversary edition.

Conan and I had spent a decade together . . . and if you had asked me at that time, I might have said that was enough. Nearly another decade later, however, I would return to Marvel (at least as a freelancer) and script another several years of **Conan the Barbarian** and its black-and-white companion mag **The Savage Sword of Conan**.

Maybe you can't exactly go home again . . . but sometimes you can revisit the old homestead for a little while.

And writing the adventures of Conan the Cimmerian is something of which I never tired.

I hope you feel the same way about reading them.

Roy Thomas has been a writer and often editor of comics since 1965— and he's still at it. But he looks back with especial fondness on his 1970–1980s scripting of the adventures of Conan.